To Becky

blessings from the Lord. Let Ephesians 3:20 be your present Word from the Lord.

If the
MOUNTAIN
Could Speak

PRAYER MOUNTAIN DALLAS

ROBERT SUMMERS

Blessings Robert

IF THE MOUNTAIN COULD SPEAK

ISBN: 0-9657997-2-7

Published by:
Prayer Mountain Press
5950 Eagle Ford Drive
Dallas, Texas 75249

Mailing Address:
P. O. Box 210733
Dallas, Texas 75211

Phone: 972-296-8919
Email: mtcreek@aol.com
Website: www.mtcreek.com

Cover Design, Art Layout and Typesetting by Michael Ruiz
Editorial and Format assistance by Verna Stutzman, M.A. (Linguistics)
Printed in The United States of America

"This shall be written for the generation to come..."
Psalm 102:18

And for visionaries and dreamers whom God has touched, laying hold on them to change their world through prayer.

DEDICATION

To my wife JoAn,
A deep well of love and encouragement.

And in memory of Mom and Dad Summers,
My most supportive fans.

"What shall I render to the Lord
For all His benefits toward me?"
Psalm 116:12

Prophetic prayer ministries arise in those crucial moments of history when all the world is astir with change. Praying people initiate transition. Spiritual revolutions turn with them. All over our nation, strong centers of prayer are emerging. Prayer steps in where politics fail. A national revival is at hand.

This is the intriguing story of Dallas Prayer Mountain. Driving up the steep lane to the top, you immediately sense both the uncommon perspective, and the Presence, the Presence of the Lord. People of all cultures find access to God here. Jesus often resorted to the mountain to pray. His followers still enjoy the same habit.

The story behind this mysterious mountain of 100 acres is miraculous. From its summit, one can view iconic landmarks of the Dallas/Fort Worth Metroplex. Looking westward across the Trinity valley, the view is dominated by giant Cowboy Stadium, The Ball Park in Arlington, Six Flags Family Park, and even the downtown Fort Worth skyline. Cedar Hill State Park, with its hills wrapping around a big lake, is the most prominent feature to the southwest. At night the northern sky is lighted by the brightness of DFW International Airport.

These episodes of faith are written here so future generations can appreciate the faithfulness of God. His grace plays a huge role, because common folk in an average size congregation accomplished this work. The Lord made the difference, evidencing the fact that "fervent, effective prayer...avails much." (James 4:16)

TABLE OF CONTENTS

FOREWORD

This is an amazing book! I have read every page. The panoramic portrayal of the Summers' journey to establish God's *Prayer Mountain* in Southwest Dallas is a refresher course in faith at work. In the reading, I do have one priceless advantage which many who will read this book do not have, something which makes this book even more wonderful to me—I have had the honor of walking alongside Robert and JoAn as they lived the story.

If The Mountain Could Speak is more than a historical review of the establishing of another ministry. It effortlessly entwines itself around both your heart and your mind. And before you realize it, you suddenly discover rich deposits of truth have become yours without even asking.

If you are a preacher, I promise that you will find enough sermon material to last through the next year. Not just illustrations, but persuasive truth and insight will touch a resonating chord in your spirit.

If you are a weary traveler, you will be refreshed as if drinking a cup of cold water on a scorching hot Texas August day. With heart and soul refreshed, you will be encouraged not only to take the next step, but to face your future with renewed confidence and vigor.

If you are a visionary, a dreamer, this book will help you give shape and form to a calling that may to this point seem perpetually just out-of-reach. Or less than crystal clear. Somewhere in these chapters you will lay hold of that special *something* which will whisper in your spirit, "*This is right…this is for me.*"

Having just completed 50 years in Christian ministry, I have been around long enough to see many things pass in and out of the church of America. The criteria for evaluation and acceptance are not universal. We have been far too gullible, too eagerly grasping, yet with inadequate discernment. What we have embraced has left us empty and tired.

It does seem to me that the American church is slowly reawakening to the need for two things: First, the voice of mature Fathers-in-the faith; Second, things real and of eternal value. We have wearied ourselves in pursuit of the flash and dash. Emptiness has compelled us to revisit *content and honesty.*

The *content* of this book is the written voice of two people who have earned the right to be heard—and followed. As a collective voice, Robert and JoAn provide a source of experience, maturity and honesty for people who want to have something real and powerful invade their Christian experience, aspiring people who are not content for it to always be *someone else's story.*

The *content* is not peripheral; it is right on target for genuine seekers who yearn for their own testimony with God. The *content* is relevant for those saints who are willing to take a chance and engage the unpredictable. It is relevant for people who have lost hope, but who just can't let go of God. It is relevant for this time, for this generation. It is *real.*

The *honesty* of success *and* failure that mark the pages of this book comes from two hearts that earnestly long for the next generation of God's servants to learn something about the faithfulness of God, which will minimize confusion of how God works. It's about God's timing, which will minimize the frustration in delayed promises. It's about God's provision, which will minimize the fear of lack.

It is *honest* about coming to grips with circumstances that seem contrary to the character of God. What do you allow yourself to think? How do you allow yourself to feel? *This is so foreign to everything you have known and been taught about Him!*

You will want to keep a pen handy. Be prepared to highlight and make marginal notes.

If The Mountain Could Speak is well written. More importantly, it is well lived.

Dr. Jim Mackey
Founder of Shepherd Springs Ministries

CHAPTER ONE

THE HEIGHTS OF THE HILLS ARE HIS

The heights of the hills are His also.
Psalm 95:4

His ways are past finding out.
Romans11:33

I was quite surprised, actually, when I first saw this high hill. It was an unexpected sight. Peering out the airplane window, I was watching the city of Dallas pass by below as our jet gained altitude. The city decreased to neighboring communities and finally disappeared into countryside. Then suddenly it was there. I saw this obviously high ridge, a long running escarpment of craggy green hills with occasional white rock bluffs. Here and there a promontory jutted out over the valley below. It was all maybe a good mile or so down below our plane.

In the golden light of early morning, I could make out the highly accented topography. There were various elevations and the glowing morning light well defined them. Here and there cuts and canyons randomly appeared as deep purple shaded furrows. The downhill wooded slopes were outlined in the darkened shadows of the dawning light.

I was caught by surprise because of my notion that all of North Texas is as flat as the old Dallas-Fort Worth turnpike. High wooded hills may be common in other geographical regions. But not here. Like rain which may come as torrents in summer in other climes, here it is a rare welcomed blessing. So also are hills.

Our passenger jet continued its climbing pattern toward Austin from Dallas Love Field. The sunlight dappled hills began to fade away. Turning to the passenger seated beside me, a business suited, executive-looking man, I inquired, "Do you live in this area?"

"Sure," he replied. "I'm from Dallas."

"I didn't know these high hills were down there," I admitted. "Do they have a name?"

He stretched to crane his neck and get a look out the window at the earth below. "Oh, those hills—they call them the Cedar Mountains," he observed, thoughtfully surveying the view. "Sometimes they are called the Chalk Hills." He sat back and continued scanning over the newspaper in his hand.

At that instant a thought was dropped into my spirit: *What a great place to build a Prayer Center for Dallas.* It was not a slow lingering word. It was more like a flash, like the instant flash of lightning coursing through my thoughts. Something in me stirred.

That Monday in early September of 1969 would be a day I will never forget. Not because of viewing these hills, but for all the reasons why I was headed down to Austin. I was en route to meet up with a miracle—one of the great miracles of my life. It was a stunning healing. This healing had brought a conclusion to a very trying, painful ordeal for my young family.

Just two weeks prior, what started as a day of happy celebration in our Houston home ended in woe and pain. On the first Sunday in September, we had received an early morning registered mail, special delivery envelope containing a check. This was a handsome amount of money, especially for young ministers who were mostly teaching in the late 1960's Jesus Movement among ex-hippies. The cashier's check was an advance payment on royalties from Fawcett World Library Premier Books, a publisher in New York City. They had contracted to publish the first book I authored, entitled *Me The Flunkie*, detailing the humorous and tragic tales of my inner city Houston high school class for drop outs. This was the largest check our young family had ever received. And we were elated. We had been surviving on a shoestring, having fun but somewhat penniless.

We would hardly have time to savor the good news though. Later that evening our eighteen month old toddler son, Kipling, was hurt in a freak accident. While crawling out of a wooden toy box in the church nursery, his foot became bound in its board side. Trying to free himself, he fell over backwards. His foot could not move in its bound position. When we pulled him out, his screams were extreme and unbearable. This was more than any plight he had previously suffered. A moment before, he had been walking. Now he wouldn't even attempt a hobble. His heart stopping cries interrupted the whole church service. In fact, his screams were so intense that he became nauseated. Whether or not we held him, he could not be comforted. Everyone gathered around to pray over the child who was beginning to convulse with his screams.

We knew something was seriously wrong.

Within the next hour, we were sitting in the emergency room of Tidelands General Hospital. There the X-ray technician had called in our family physician, Dr. Robert McAmis. They pored over the X-rays together, then asked us to step in and view the X-ray report. Our boy had suffered a major spiral break, a very bad broken leg. If anybody could help our hurting child, Dr. McAmis could. The day had begun on a thrilling high. Now we were plummeting down a long, painful corridor of tears and bad news.

Our beautiful baby boy faced a long hospitalization, strung up in cables and weights traction for at least six weeks. Both legs needed to be up, we were informed, because of the rapid growth rate of his age group. Six weeks! This crying, nauseous child was then strung upside down— looking like a side of beef hung up in a butcher shop. Due to the traction, we could not hold him in our arms to comfort him. We were praying every gut wrenching moment for a miracle. All the while we labored to console the little upside down pain wracked child. How do you explain what has happened to his world? He had only three or four words in his vocabulary. He cried them out, "Mommy, Dadda, Nanna!" We endured a lot. We prayed a lot. We held on to God.

His Nanna came as quickly as she could. JoAn was at Kip's side almost every minute. Visitors came by. They offered condolences and prayers and toys. Some came by just to gawk at the sight. In the small hospital, the upside down boy was a main attraction.

A week and a half after the accident I had to board a plane for Midland, Texas. I had long been scheduled to be a visiting teacher there in the public schools health classes. My experience with inner city teenagers and drug addictions had resulted in many calls to lecture in high school assembly programs as well as in the classroom. In my absence, God was at work. In fact in Midland a strong group of prayer intercessors began fervently praying with us for a miracle.

In the hospital room, the upside down boy was beginning to adjust. One night twelve or thirteen days into the ordeal, JoAn felt a warm and comforting sensation that the Lord was healing our boy. "Jesus, if this is You, I need to know," she prayed.

First thing the next morning, she called our doctor to ask for an x-ray. He was kind but firm. "At this point, it's still too early," he answered her. "The x-ray would be a waste of time and money."

She persisted. She even offered to pay for it out of pocket. He finally agreed, repeating his caveat that we should not expect much. And sure enough, the new x-ray he ordered showed nothing positive. But JoAn was unmoved in her faith. It was a big test for her. In her own words, she recounted the struggle to keep holding on to God in the face of all this bad news. She had recorded the long hospital ordeal in her journal.

The technician made the x-ray. The results were exactly what the doctor had predicted. My hopes plummeted into despair. Robert had to leave for a ministry trip. Mother had to return home after two weeks of helping me. I was left alone to cope with this.

After crooning Kip to sleep that night, I crumpled before the Lord. Finally I stopped demanding my own way. I prayed what Catherine Marshall called 'The Prayer of Relinquishment' in her book Beyond Our Selves. This is where you just let go of what you really want, throw yourself on the Lord's mercy, and say, "Not my will, but Thine."

Alright, Lord, I have done everything I know to do. I have prayed, believed, called others to join their faith with mine, insisted on the x-ray in the face of my doctor's obvious disapproval. I've tried everything I know to try and nothing has worked. Here we are still facing four more weeks of this miserable hospital life. I give up, Lord. If You want us to endure another month here, then I simply ask for Your grace to get us through. Be with us, Lord, because I cannot make it on my own. My strength is gone. And I sat there before Him, totally spent.

Sounds of sobbing wafted into the room, floating in from across the hall. Compassion welled in me, for I had shed many tears myself in those past few days. I quietly rose, followed the sounds of grief, and entered the room where a woman lay weeping. Walking to her bedside, I softly asked, "Why are you crying? Can I help?"

Quickly she turned to me in the dim light. "Oh, I am so afraid," she cried. "I'm having surgery in the morning and I'm just so scared!"

"Would you like me to pray for you?" I asked.

"Oh yes, please," she gasped, like a drowning woman grasping a lifeline.

I laid my hand gently on her shoulder and began to pray. As I asked the Lord to send the Comforter to her, I felt her begin to calm. I spoke Psalm 23 softly, "Yea, though I walk through the valley of the shadow of death, I will fear no evil: for thou art with me; thy rod and they staff they comfort me…Surely goodness and mercy shall follow me all the days of my life…" By the time I said Amen, she was totally at peace.

She looked up at me wonderingly and whispered, "Are you an angel?"

I smiled. "No, I'm the lady across the hall whose little boy is strung up in traction. Now get some rest. The Lord is with you."

During that brief encounter when I reached out to help someone else, something wondrous happened in my baby's room. Just three days later enough calcium deposits had formed in Kip's leg that he was released from the hospital! Three days instead of four weeks! God gave us our miracle when I focused outward to someone in need, when I became a channel for His goodness.[1]

Dr. McAmis did something very unusual. He came in on Sunday, his one day off. He wanted to check up on our son Kip. "I didn't sleep much last night," he told JoAn, acting a bit as if he knew something we didn't know. "Let's do another x-ray on Kip's leg," he offered somewhat hopefully.

As soon as he saw the x-ray, he exclaimed, "Well, look at this! This is great! The calcium deposits are perfect. The break is covered over. It's healed. I'm sending this boy home today."[2] JoAn and the doctor returned to Kip's room to take him down out of traction. She held her little boy tightly for the first time in two weeks. Kip was puzzled, but happy. Doctors' orders were that Kip must stay off his feet for at least another week.

I got the phone call early Sunday before I was to speak to a large church crowd. JoAn was ecstatic with thanksgiving. The church had been praying for us. The folks were so excited they gave an offering to cover the expense of bringing JoAn and Kip out to join me in Midland. My parents had scheduled a business appointment in Austin for Monday morning. They offered to lead JoAn and Kip all the way from Houston to Austin International Airport. We would connect there and drive on out to Midland.

I was happy and thankful as our plane hastened over the Texas countryside toward Austin. I did not ponder much on sighting this big hill. After all, JoAn was awaiting me with Kip, our miracle boy. With my parents, all of us together at the airport, we would celebrate the goodness of the Lord—and His healing power.

Walking into that terminal in Austin International is one of the cherished moments of my life. More than a reunion, it was a spiritual moment. There were hugs and kisses of course. But the attention was on the child held in JoAn's arms. The leg which was broken and crippled was now whole. I took Kip up in my arms and held him tight. He had not seen his dad in days. With his big, dark, searching eyes, he was carefully checking me out. Then suddenly his face broke out into a big grin of delight. In that wonderful moment of giddy joy we were all children, drinking in the love our Father had bestowed on us.

Later I would occasionally revisit the idea of a Prayer Center in the hills of Southwest Dallas. It was more a thought down deep in my spirit rather than the musings of my mind. The concept of a Prayer Center was more like a puzzle. I did not yet have all the pieces. So I don't recall forming any opinion or visualization in my mind. Even Dallas itself was an enigma to me. I had no business connection with any ministry there. My only association with Dallas was the fond memory of my late grandmother. She had lived her life there. She had been a woman of faith and prayer, interceding for that city.

Sometimes the heavenly vision comes to us as a still, small voice, sent for our consideration. If we pause to ponder it, then it will linger. For this we must turn aside, as Moses *turned aside to behold the burning bush*. Our world would be a very different world if Moses had not turned aside. Although we may never hear a thundering voice, we can expect the leadings and drawings of the Lord for us will be sure. Uncanny perhaps, but also unmistakable are His ways. The voice of the Shepherd is distinct. His sheep know His voice. I heard a Word that day. I did not understand. Maybe later I would have the key to make it more than a passing thought.

God is fractal in His dealings with men. By this I mean He hides His movements and conceals His strategies much like a skilled chess player. He does not obligate Himself to reveal His ways to the disinterested and unresponsive. But to those who will turn aside, who will seize the moment, He makes plain His will and purpose.

In the words of the psalmist David: "He made known His ways to Moses, His acts to the children of Israel."[3]

To understand, to perceive the ways of God is a gift. Moses knew *why* God did what He did in carrying out Israel's deliverance. The children of Israel only knew the *what* of the matter. God had a good plan, albeit a hidden plan for me. The day would come when I would know why the Lord seated me in that particular seat by the window on the east side of that Austin bound jetliner. He had a reason for showing me this mountain on that special day of celebration.

"For I know the plans I have for you," declares the Lord, "plans to prosper you and not to harm you, plans to give you a hope and a future."
Jeremiah 29:11

" ...the mystery of God, both of the Father and of Christ, in whom are hidden all the treasures of wisdom and knowledge."
Colossians 2:2,3

"I do not know how the great loving Father will bring out light at last, but he knows, and he will do it."
–David Livingstone, Scottish missionary to Africa

CHAPTER TWO

THE SIGN

Lord, You have been our dwelling place in all generations.
Before the mountains were brought forth,
Or ever You had formed the earth and the world,
Even from everlasting to everlasting, You are God.
Psalm 90:1,2

Got any rivers you think are uncrossable? Got any mountains you can't
tunnel through? God specializes in things thought impossible And He will do
what no other power can do. (an old Camp Meeting chorus)

God will pull you through—if you can stand the pull. –W.P. Jones

The year was 1980. I wiped my sweaty hands on my jeans and crawled through the rusted barbed wire fence while my friend held up the top wire. A light rain, cool and fresh, was falling over Dallas.

Today my attention had been captured by an unexpected visitor. A close buddy had appeared at our front door. But much to my surprise, this fellow pastor, Cleddie Keith, was too stirred in his spirit to come into our house. He had caught a glimpse of some kind of other worldly vision while praying and driving his car from Fort Worth to Dallas. Cleddie is one of those rare servants of the Lord who amazingly manages to stupefy your rational mind and puzzle you beyond comfortable limits. He's usually right on. I felt today was one of those moments. Prophetic moments, I call them. God moments.

"Got any mountains, any hills in this area?" he quizzed me as I opened the door to receive him. "Let's go drive out there."

"Yeah, sure," I answered. "But, hey Cleddie, it's raining. Come on in out of the rain," I urged. "I can show you the hills later." I wondered how he knew about the hills of Southwest Dallas. Most people have no idea. I urged my friend again, "Come on in, Cleddie."

He balked. Cleddie insisted I come riding with him. He wanted to tell me something about "a hill" and I really needed to come with him. Now.

At his urging I pulled on my boots and headed out with him. He began driving and excitedly asking me where were the hills? He had obviously had a strong experience. He was telling me what he had just seen in the

Spirit. It was like a vision, involving a detailed panorama. In this scenario, he had seen me teaching at the front of a good-sized lecture hall. He could see that I was engrossed in instructing students. This particular room featured raised tiered seating, lecture hall style, with ascending levels. Students were busily taking down notes as I spoke.

He was struck by this room's wonderful view. On both his right and on his left were large picture windows. To his right Cleddie glimpsed a large blue lake which he could see stretching for miles away toward the far horizon. Out the left side windows he saw a wooded creek bottom. The big panoramic view suggested he was up high, overlooking a valley.

He continued to draw a clear visual scenario. I could tell he was stirred, even awed. "Robert," he told me, "you were writing on a board behind you. I could see the words you wrote. *You can't split an eagle's tongue and teach it to say—Eagle wants a cracker!*" I chuckled. But Cleddie was speaking in a considerably serious tone.

Cleddie intuited that in this scene he visualized I was engaged in a teaching on leadership. Amazingly, this whole image was so real to him, so clearly depicted, that he was sure he had seen something of the future. He felt compelled to find that mountain. He wanted to lay claim to it. Rain or no rain. I marked that there was absolutely no "perhaps" or "maybe" in his demeanor. Cleddie is a man of strong convictions. That place existed. But how could we find such a place?

As Cleddie drove, I rehearsed to him how I had viewed out the airplane window over ten years ago a unique promontory. We discussed the fact that, remarkable as it seems, I am now living only five or six miles from that very same ridge of high hills. Maybe I had failed to realize that God was always moving us closer, inevitably, to the hills we were now driving through. After ministering in church camps set in the Rockies, smaller hills no longer captured my attention as in days gone by.

Cleddie and I had both experienced a wide degree of travels, flowing with the revival streams of the Jesus Movement. JoAn and I had spent all summer of 1971 in Southern California. There we connected with many spiritual leaders who greatly influenced our lives. Then in the fall of 1971 we moved to the Dallas/Fort Worth area to work with David Wilkerson in preparation for the big *Explo '72*. This was a well-planned gathering of over

175,000 college age radical Christians at Dallas' Fair Park. The event was a multi-organizational effort led by Bill Bright and Campus Crusade for Christ. Billy Graham concluded the convocation with a huge outdoor rally.

JoAn and I had been occupied in that fruitful season developing new printed material for discipleship training of young Christians. We turned out large volumes of material, printing them at Lindsay Press at Christ for the Nations in Dallas. Not long after, Gordon Lindsay, founder and magazine editor of *Christ for the Nations,* unexpectedly passed away. We were recruited into the CFN editorial offices. JoAn was charged with editing and publishing in book form many of the manuscript Bible studies now left unpublished by the late Gordon Lindsay. JoAn and I oversaw the *Christ for the Nations* magazine design and publication.

We had always dreamed of living in the Texas Hill Country. Commuting on weekends from Dallas, we assisted my parents in planting a new church congregation of mostly retired folk at Canyon Lake, a resort village near San Antonio. Amazingly, this young church quickly filled up with youthful Jesus People, ex-hippies who now in their words were "saved, shaved, and well-behaved." To minister to this new wave of the congregation, we finally moved to Canyon Lake in the summer of 1976. We developed a local Bible School known as Wildwood School. Some of these young people became missionaries. Others became respected businessmen and craftsmen. We put four hard years, good years, into Wildwood. How often the young believers and I resorted to a mountain to pray, sometimes remaining there all night. Prayer sustained us. It was not easy dealing with ex-druggies from dysfunctional families and backgrounds of sexual promiscuity.

We also continued commuting back and forth to California. JoAn had begun producing *Backyard*, a children's television program seen on Trinity Broadcasting Network and later on the Christian Broadcasting Network. Our cast of twelve players all lived in the greater Los Angeles area. Through the '70s we must have made over 60 trips for this colorful, fun-filled production. *Backyard* was seen in most major viewing areas of the country.

In 1980 we felt strongly led to move back to Dallas. The DFW airport was more convenient for national and international travel. Also we had an effective open door to teach Bible in North Dallas, in the growing home prayer meeting hosted by one of Dallas' civic leaders and major developers, Jim Williams, and his wife Nedra.

By now our family had grown to include a budding young artist and writer, Rod Butler, who was a true older brother to our son Kip. Rod was a gifted creator of puppet shows. He enjoyed assisting us with the *Backyard* children's television production. Together we all packed up a U-Haul truck and moved back to Dallas. Our secretary at Wildwood handed us a special last minute "going away" gift. It was a book, the classic daily devotional, *Streams in the Desert* compiled by Mrs. Charles Cowman. It was fitting, now as I look back, that we began life in Dallas with our early morning family devotional from that book's January 1 scripture reading: *The land whither ye go to possess, it is a land of hills and valleys and drinketh water of the rain of heaven: a land which the Lord thy God careth for: the eyes of the Lord are always upon it, from the beginning of the year even unto the end of the year.*[4] Our prayer times together were rich and reassuring, and especially needed. We had arrived penniless in Dallas. We had expended ourselves on the Wildwood ministry. We needed a change.

So by spring of 1980, our focus was back in Dallas. We knew our future lay here. Cleddie and I reminisced as he drove the car as close as he could possibly get to the hills. Most of the chain of big rolling ridges stood on a sprawling, derelict ranch. No houses. No roads. No access. In the middle of this ranch, a mule ranch I later learned, was a winding overgrown ranch road. This was little more than a Jeep trail, which led to a protruding high hill that Cleddie was interest in exploring.

I tore my rain soaked trousers that day crawling through barbed wire fences attempting to get closer to that hill. We joked that we were like pioneer prospectors searching for gold. Because of the rain, Cleddie and I finally had to abandon our spur-of- the-moment expedition. Heading back to our house for coffee, Cleddie talked more plainly about his "vision." It would surely come. Though it tarry, if we have to wait for it, it would surely come. He was convinced.

I now believed it. I was still hoping for some tangible sign. But I began to write down the vision for others to read. I began to speak it. A prayer and retreat center in the hills of Southwest Dallas. The burden resonated in my spirit. It would be staffed with praying, visionary saints. This would be their mission, their service to Dallas-Fort Worth and the world.

Meanwhile, our North Dallas prayer group had become a growing congregation, too large for private homes to accommodate. We would soon move to an old Episcopal church facility, Saint Thomas the Apostle Church. A dear elderly Episcopal priest, Father Guy Usher, invited our group into his well-located chapel. We continued to be blessed with enlargement. Especially after this fine old rector gave us the eleven o'clock Sunday morning service. Kirk and Deby Dearman led worship. They were popular composers of many Charismatic era worship anthems, such as "We Bring the Sacrifice of Praise" and "To Thee We Ascribe Glory."

By 1984 however, I was wrestling over direction for our congregation's future. The Bishop and Church Counsel had forced our friend Guy Usher to retire. He was replaced by a liberal priest who wanted no group in the Episcopal Church who practiced Spirit-filled worship and divine healing services. The new man wanted Saint Thomas to become a religious center for gay community activism. We were forced to move our congregation out to a Dallas civic auditorium. Tragically, St. Thomas Church was the site of 42 AIDS related funerals the first nine months after we left. This was the report from Father Guy Usher.

In September of 1984, a young, artistic former pastor named Stuart began visiting our services. He was presently unemployed as a creator of high dollar wood carved signs. JoAn and I had been planning to order a sign for our renovated Hill Country cottage, a small sign we would hang over the front door welcoming tired guests who retreated there. The simple sign, reflecting our own yearning for a start on our bigger vision, would read *Prayer Mountain, Welcome*.

Knowing Stuart's need, we advanced him an ample amount of money to get him started on a sign. When he completed the project, he brought the sign to our Sunday service to make something of a presentation. He had it under wraps.

He apologized for its large, oversized dimensions. As he unveiled it, he carefully explained why it was so big. "I felt compelled by the Lord," Stuart clarified. "I started on a small sign. But the Lord told me that wouldn't do. 'Make it big, Stuart!' He said. 'They will need a large sign.'" It was big! Very big.

In my private prayers I had been asking the Lord for a sign of His leading us to finally begin to establish the Prayer Center in Southwest

Dallas. Now, inescapable, in front of us all, was a giant-sized, beautiful carved wooden sign replete with gilded stand-out lettering which read,

PRAYER MOUNTAIN
WELCOME

Stuart had indeed heard the Lord on this project. I was stunned. Amazed. I remember silently thanking the Lord and pondering, *Lord, I asked You for a sign. You have given me a literal sign.* It was much too large to attach to our front door. It would have to be positioned prominently on a mountain. Somewhere in those high hills.

We all sensed this was like the Lord's earnest of more to come. The congregation applauded and praised the Lord. Stuart was relieved, now sure that he had heard the Lord.

God was up to something that day. My burden was transitioning. My grace for North Dallas was lifting. I was now thinking of Southwest Dallas. Some of our leading families had already moved down into that general area, wanting to raise their families away from the highly congested and busy northern part of the city. As my focus was shifting, I knew I must find that mountain. But it was still a mystery to me. How would we access it? There would be many obstacles to overcome.

In October of 1984, Cleddie Keith and I were asked to inaugurate Prayer Mountain in Shepherdsville, Kentucky. It was a new ministry of Waymon and Bob Rogers, father and son pastors from Louisville, Kentucky. While visiting in their new mountain retreat, I felt the clearest leading in my spirit: return to Texas and fully devote my energies to developing Prayer Mountain Dallas.

When I arrived home, I prayed with JoAn about the first step to take. We were led by the Spirit to visit my Uncle Joe Summers, the patriarch and oldest member of the Summers family. He was a retired new car dealer in Duncanville, a Dallas suburb. We felt we needed the patriarch's blessing—although Uncle Joe was much more a businessman than spiritual leader.

We would be surprised to have that notion shattered, the idea we held of Uncle Joe's spiritual lack. He quickly grasped our request for the patriarch's spoken blessing over our vision. He began to pray over us. Imagine our amazement. Then quite unexpectedly an anointing came upon the old businessman. He shook. His voice quivered, then grew loud as if he were prophesying: "Yes. Yes. There will be a Prayer Mountain on the hills. A Prayer Mountain that the Lord will raise up. Yes, I see it now. There is a mountain waiting for you. Be bold. The Lord is with you. Yes. Yes." He concluded by asking the Holy Spirit to open our eyes as Elisha prayed for his servant to see the armies of Heaven surrounding them to fight for the prophet. There was not a dry eye in the house.

We were absolutely stunned. The huge surprise was that this reference to Prayer Mountain came from Uncle Joe Summers rather than some seasoned preacher. This was singularly unusual for a man who had not shown great interest in spiritual matters. He was well known in civic circles and in business chambers. We left his house that day thoroughly convinced of the Spirit's hand upon us. We got the blessing just in time. We buried Uncle Joe two months later. The encouragement he spoke continued to echo in our hearts, clear and easy to understand. The Lord is never vague. He was drawing us inexorably to the higher ground of Southwest Dallas.

The Lord God is my strength,
He will make my feet like deer's feet
And He will make me walk on my high hills.
Habakkuk 3:19

The fitness of the Christian miracles, and their difference from these mythological
miracles, lies in the fact that they show invasion by a Power which is not alien.
–C.S. Lewis, *Miracles*

CHAPTER THREE

GIVE ME THIS MOUNTAIN!

...give me this mountain of which the Lord spoke in that day.
Caleb in Joshua 14:12

For every mountain You've brought me over
For every trial You've seen me through
For every blessing, Hallelujah!
For this I give You praise.
(chorus from *"For Every Mountain"* by Kurt Carr)

The increasing, loud chop-chop-chop of the approaching helicopter grew almost deafening. The big whirring bird circled and slowly descended to the ground. The wind whipped through my hair. I glanced over the crowd. Many of them were waiting, as I was, to be airlifted up over a 3500 acre ranch, a hilly spread, which was to become Dallas' largest-ever new subdivision. Standing there with me was Al Block, Vice President of the colossal community development company that planned this big project. He had offered to take me aloft to view what they envisioned to become The Villages of Mountain Creek. They were already advertising this planned development as the Dallas Hill Country.

I knew this was big. Today's promotion cost a lot of money.

The launching of this new enterprise was done up in such a way that epitomized the way Dallas does business. Our city and county officials were all there, along with other dignitaries. The developer's engineers and architects had presented bold concepts and plans to the City Council for the construction of a new city of sixty thousand residents. No detail, no bit of terrain was overlooked. Everything was mapped and drawn in for neighborhoods, schools, ball fields, parks, ponds, roads, bridges, and corporate office buildings and warehouses. Everything was planned to the smallest feature—everything except church facility sites. I had made a point of this lack when asked to address the Council.

To make up for this oversight, the company's Vice President Al Block, had offered to take me up and give me an aerial view of the best likely site to construct a chapel. So we ducked our heads low and ran to the aircraft. Clambering aboard the helicopter, we buckled into our seats and prepared for lift off. With the noisy revving of the engine, we were off and away. We headed south over Interstate 20. Then the pilot turned westward to give us a bird's eye view of a vast graded area where the U.S. Army Corps of Engineers had employed giant earth moving machinery, busy at work creating Dallas' newest 8000 acre lake and reservoir. A four mile long dam was now stretching across Mountain Creek valley. After a quick flyover our pilot headed our craft eastward over the new development.

A minute or so later, Al Block was tapping me on the shoulder. He was pointing down at a wooded promontory, an outcropped ridge which was jutting out from the rest of the chain of hills which ran undulating in a southwesterly direction. What made this ridge distinct from the others was its striking white bluff face. As my eyes scanned over the site below, I was stunned by the realization I was gazing at the very same rugged hill I had spotted on my flight from Dallas down to Austin fifteen years earlier. Al Block, above the roar of the engine, was explaining that this was his preference of all places for building a chapel. My heartbeat quickened with excitement while my eyes pored over the site. I could make out a narrow, winding ranch trail which followed the ridge upward to the top of the high hill. That helped me identify the hill as the same location that Cleddie Keith and I had tried to reach on that rainy day six years earlier. Now at last I mused, "I am here." I was looking right down on this same hill which first attracted my attention years ago, long before I had any real connections in Dallas. I recalled the words impressed on my mind that day: *a great site for a Prayer Center*. It was as if I were standing in front of a lighted map in the center of a huge mall where a big pointed arrow declares, YOU ARE HERE. *I am here*, I thought. *Thank God Almighty, I am here!*

Then before I knew it, the helicopter was turning back north and heading back to the big party tents at the new ranch headquarters. Other people, mostly civic dignitaries and home builders were awaiting their turn in the air.

As I drove my car the few miles back to the house to tell JoAn what I had seen, my mind flashed back to an experience which had impacted me more than I realized. I was only six years old. Our family was on an outing, a fireside youth fellowship and wiener roast in a piney woods county park near Houston. Night had fallen. The play of the congregation's children was broken by a call to come gather around the campfire. We scampered back to the adults positioned by the fire. I could hear my father's beckoning call as I made my way back. Then suddenly I was momentarily halted by a beautiful sight which somehow also conveyed sentiment, or maybe Presence, to me. I was transfixed as I stared at the outline of a very comely big hill bathed in the moonlight. I recall that in an unusual way I perceived that this sight was a special sign to me, that what I was seeing had meaning: the big moon and the iridescent hill in the night sky. I did not linger in this encounter. In a moment it was over as I recall hearing my father bidding us hurry along to the fire pit. Yet the effect of that brief miracle would linger with me. What did I see? And why?

Later, growing up as a teenager in Houston, I occasionally flashed back on the experience of that church fireside devotional. It had to be a miraculous apparition I had seen, some supernatural sign. It had to be. The fact is, there are really no such hills within more than a hundred miles of Houston's Gulf Coastal flatlands. There exists not even a rolling swell of terrain in the whole of Harris County—where we picnicked at the time.

Yet the result of that fleeting childhood encounter would influence my enthusiastic connection with hills. Much later I would find myself giving more than a passing glance to every high hill which came into view. It was a bit more like close scrutiny. There was something like a magnetic attraction drawing my eyes to inspect or to *study* what others may have never even noticed about some distant hill on the horizon. It really was not a compulsive thing. But perhaps I deemed hills a more valuable consideration than others did. Every hill climb was an adventure to me, wanting to capture the view from every mountain top.

The result was that in High School I pored over topographical maps. In college I excelled in geology studies, and eventually became something of a professor's assistant. I trace that back to my childhood vision out in the park.

Arriving back at our house, I brought JoAn up to speed on what had transpired in my helicopter ride. That was the day she and I knew for sure that the new church congregation we were planting, Mountain Creek Community Church, would someday have its meeting hall on that mountain top. I purposed to immediately return and hike over that location on foot. The term *prayer center* now reverberated in my spirit.

When we began this new church plant, we were persuaded that it should be known for its prayer—a house of prayer. Well known men of God spoke encouragement over us and this concept. Cleddie Keith, Des Evans, Robert Terrell, DeVern Fromke, Bob Willhite, Leonard Ravenhill, and E.M.Fjordbak all exhorted us to be genuine God seekers. A praying church.

The next morning, a beautiful North Texas spring day dawned bright and clear. I hurriedly wolfed down a bite of breakfast and hastened out to explore what I had seen yesterday from the air.

Driving to the end of city roads, I parked the car and hiked the remaining mile to that hill. The ranch road I followed wound its way through thickets of cedar, cactus, and mesquite in a landscape brushed with patches of bright blue fields of bluebonnets. The fragrant air was brisk, almost intoxicating. A meadowlark sang nearby. Up in the sky two small scissortails were in a dispute with a much larger red-tailed hawk chasing him away in a daring show of pluckiness. The scissortail's valiant action always reminds me of a fearless little David taking on a great big giant Goliath.

I set a brisk pace as I hastened up that rough, overgrown ranch road that followed close by a rusted barbed wire fence. It led through tall grass and bright patches of wild flowers. Then the road came to a fork. The right fork veered and led through a well-worn fence gap conspicuous for its stout but weathered old cedar posts. The trail dipped around the foot of the hill then ascended steeply upward.

I was now on a rough bulldozed jeep trail that was mercilessly eroded with washouts. No small vehicle could navigate its deep ruts. I headed up toward the bluff, surveying the place. Enthusiasm spurred me into a faster pace. Soon I was practically jogging. Little did I then realize that soon I would be engaged in the struggle of my life. The scissortails' fearless scramble to intercept the hawk, the showdown of the little contesting the very big would become the pattern for our next few years. The contest would require much more than pluck and nerve. The battle would be a spiritual one, fought not in the skies, but prayerfully fought in the higher heavens. It would require a people of devoted intercession and spiritual warfare. A holy, praying, faithful company.

At the top of the hill only one small window, a clearing in the thicket, allowed for a clear perspective. In the distance, a cloud of dust arose from the area where giant earthmovers were crisscrossing the sloped sides of the big earthen dam. On the far horizon the skyline of downtown Fort Worth some twenty-five miles west could be seen.

The rest of the summit was almost totally blanketed by a thick canopy of briar vines. Most of the trees were younger regrowth trees, maybe only ten years old. They were struggling toward maturity, enmeshed by the pervasive briar. Poison ivy was everywhere in abundance. In a small clearing on the uphill side of the road, some rocks were stacked up and set in alignment of some kind of order. A campfire of sorts, I first thought. No. Upon second glance, the arrangement of the stones suggested something else. More like an altar. An altar! Way out here? I pondered this question as I carefully considered what this site meant. At the moment I had no idea that this high place had been frequented by witches. We would later discover people of the Dark Side wanted this high ground as much as we did. And they would let us know.

There was not much opportunity to check out any of the off trail areas. The net of thick briar was truly impenetrable. So I headed back down. Near the foot of the hill, the trail ran through a grassy glade and under a shady elm grove. There I sat down in the tall grass to pray. The bower of green limbs made a temple of sorts for me.

I felt inadequate—like a child who was too short of vocabulary to fully express himself. "How do you ask for a mountain?" I questioned. "How do I pray?"

Then the famous words of faithful Caleb in the Book of Joshua, the elderly man who petitioned Joshua, came to mind: *Give me this mountain*! It was a simple enough prayer. I could pray that.

Only God would know how we could get this property. But I suddenly sensed we should have this mountain. God's purposes and our very destiny were wrapped up in this beautiful hill.

Faith began to arise in my heart as I prayed. There in the grass on the sloping hillside I began to hear a promise reverberate in my spirit. It was the Lord's Word in Matthew 17:20: "If you have faith as a mustard seed, you will say to this mountain, 'Move from here to there,' and it will move; and nothing will be impossible for you."

It was as if the Lord were coaching me from His Word, *You can move a mountain!* Honestly, the encounter was a sacred moment for me. Under the spreading shade of those big elms, I began to know that the dream of Prayer Mountain would be incarnated, fleshed out, a reality. The Lord will do it. Hope was like a pilot light igniting a big flame of faith within. I lingered in that place.

One of my favorite Bible stories has always been the episode of Jacob's dream of the ladder to heaven. Jacob was so impressed, he gave the place the name of *Bethel,* God's house. His words became immortalized in story and song. "Surely the Lord is in this place, and I did not know it…How awesome is this place! This is none other than the house of God, and this is the gate of heaven!"[5]

All these things I pondered as I headed back to my car. To me the Word of God is far more penetrating than mere thoughts. It is the predominating, guiding force in my life. When the Holy Spirit illuminates God's Word, He also helps me hide it away in my heart. I've learned to trust His guidance. The promises of God are His word of honor. He is faithful to His Word. He had told my soul something I would never forget.

Later that day a young worship leader in our congregation drove up from Baylor University. He was raring to go see the mountain. Together we were hiking back up the mountain. We were suddenly challenged by a rattlesnake of considerable size coiled in the trail. He defied us to tread any further. I have no quarrel with rattlesnakes—but I really don't like snakes that defy us. I picked up a large stone to even the odds of the contest. He rattled. I threw that rock at him, aiming to befuddle him or shoo him off the road. "In the Name of the Lord," I announced with a sportscaster's enthusiasm. Much to my surprise, the stone found its mark. Bulls-eye! Dead ringer, right on the ugly viper's head. He writhed, crooked and contorted beyond description, then suddenly bellied up. We kept a safe distance back for at least a minute to be sure he was dead. We probed his still carcass with a stick. Nothing. He was cold-cocked dead.

My young friend Jerry was absolutely amazed. I was too. When I was younger I had shot many water moccasins with a .22 caliber pistol. A garden hoe has also been a handy weapon I have used to behead dangerous pit vipers. But never before have I flat out stoned a rattlesnake. This was a first! That ugly snake died with his forked tongue hanging out. We walked on.

Jerry as always saw some great theological truth in the snake incident. Our conversation was especially amusing as we hiked up the hill. By the time we reached the summit, our talk was more thought provoking. "The battle is the Lord's," we concluded. It is God alone who can guide the rock to its mark. It is the Lord who bruised the serpent's head. Jerry recalled a new praise song about this. If only he had brought along his guitar. We could sing: "Through our God we shall do valiantly, for it is He who shall tread down our enemies."[6]

We wanted that mountain. But we now knew that we would have to fight the good fight for it. It would not be easy. Back home that evening JoAn and I had a lot to think and pray about. Following the admonition of Habakkuk 2:2 we began to "write the vision…and make it plain, so that he may run who reads it." We would begin to herald the message. God will bring it to pass. That is His mountain. He was there before us.

"Before the mountains were settled, Before the hills,
I was brought forth… I was there."
Proverb 8:25, 27

God is virtually begging us to ask for great things! –David Wilkerson, founder of
Teen Challenge and author of *The Cross and the Switchblade*

CHAPTER FOUR

SPEAKS TO MOUNTAINS

I say to you, if you have faith as a mustard seed,
you will say to this mountain,
"Move from here to there," and it will move
and nothing will be impossible for you.
Matthew 17:20

No one dare be so rash as to seek to do the impossible unless he has first
been empowered by the God of the impossible.
–A.W. Tozer[7]

I would often explain to my friends what I knew about the hill's geological facts. It was formed by an ancient fault line. In geological terms it is known as an ancient mountain, now greatly worn down with time. The fault line runs from Northeast Oklahoma down through Dallas to Waco. It is known as the Ouachita Fault (pronounced Washitah, with emphasis on the first syllable *Wash.*) It is visible here and there in intermittent upthrusts. Where it is the most conspicuous elevation, from the old Eagle Ford crossing of the Trinity River in Dallas down to Waco, it is referred to as the White Rock Escarpment. But the pioneer settlers just called it the Cedar Mountains.

This region of rugged ravines and rocky hills is the habitat of a wide variety of wildlife. Bobcats, coyotes, wolves, foxes, raccoons, armadillos, and turkeys roam along its ridges and green forest slopes. The escarpment is even better known for its birds. The rare and reclusive Golden-cheeked Warbler and the Black-capped Vireo—both protected songbirds—make their home here. The year we began focusing on the mountain, 1985, the Dallas City Council created an ordinance naming the downhill slopes of the escarpment as an ecologically sensitive zone. It is a refuge from urban development. This greenbelt is known as the Dallas Parks Escarpment Zone. This ordinance created a buffer whereby our immediate neighbors will only be animals of the forest.

Eventually the development company, working from the Escarpment Zone surveys, offered the hilltop five acres at a price of $175,000.00. That was a lot of money for a small beginning congregation like ours to pay.

Especially since we had begun from Day One with a major missionary commitment. At the time we were secretly and busily engaged in the old Communist ruled Eastern Bloc nations of the Soviet Union, as well as Bible translation work.

We did not have a lot of cash on hand. But with enthusiastic, sacrificial giving and a host of yard sales, we quickly came up with the twenty percent down payment. JoAn and her mom Eva raised almost $5000 of that amount by putting on a grand-sized Mexican dinner evening event. It succeeded beyond our expectations. It seemed the whole community turned out to help us raise the money for the mountain. JoAn was dog tired but happy with the results.

Our credibility in the community grew. The assurance of the vision became more solidified as the congregation prayed over the $35,000 cashier's check made out to the developer. We could assume we were well on our way to owning that mountain. It would be a relief to finally have a physical address. We were so often asked *where was our church*. It is an unfortunate mindset in our suburban American culture that to be a *real church* you have to own a physical place with a church building on it. We certainly were already doing the ministry of the Body of Christ. We were supporting missions, aiding the poor and broken, standing up for righteous causes, making disciples, and equipping saints. From the first, we were challenged by spiritual leaders to proceed with the work of the Lord and not focus on a building project as our cause for existing.

We were meeting in a rented hall at the International Linguistics Center (Wycliffe Bible Translators) on Camp Wisdom Road in Dallas. In the meantime we also came together in strong and spiritually rewarding house churches. Still, it was part of our written vision to own that mountaintop. The Linguistics Center was on a hilltop just next door to property we sought to obtain. We continued walking over that distinct high ground and praying as if we had title deed to it. The walk of faith was stretching all of us.

But then came a stunning blow! It knocked the wind out of our new-felt optimism. After a silence of almost a month, we were informed by a note in the mail that the company had rejected our offer! Only a terse explanation was attached to the returned cashier's check. A handwritten note, puzzling to be sure, seemed to carry the impression of contempt or scorn. All it said was, "Not ready to transact business with the church." We were crushed, shattered. Numb. Dumbfounded. The sales director of this company was a man I had already encountered in all my visits and correspondence. His name was Mr. Pearce. In our conversations, I had felt he was a bit cold and self-possessed. But I did not expect he would be a major problem. I had gathered from our conversations he was a Mormon (Latter Day Saint) from Ogden, Utah, educated at Brigham Young University (BYU) in Provo, Utah. I knew his home area well. As a college freshman I had spent part of a summer working with a mission for down-and-outers in Provo. I was aware that some Mormon citizens were not terribly excited about young missionaries of other faiths working in their home state of Utah. But our small team also was pleased to find that they were for the most part civil, respectful, if not friendly.

I had mingled freely with BYU students at their favorite eating places. I had more than once hiked up Provo Canyon and even climbed up partway to the top of famous Timpanogos Peak which overlooks Utah Valley. On several occasions we had gone up at night on that high hill behind BYU, known by locals as The Bench, to view the city and pray over it. That is my most intense recollection of that summer. It remains with me like a beloved souvenir, the memory of the lights of the city and Utah Lake to the west glistening in the moonlight. I had visited services in the Salt Lake City Tabernacle just to hear the Mormon Tabernacle Choir sing. All these experiences I had in common with the sales director, Mr. Pearce. We both shared a love for Utah's iconic places. I counted Latter Day Saints folk among my friends.

So it would not be unusually awkward for me to head over to his sales office for a friendly visit. This time, the sales director was plainly cold and ill at ease with me. He answered with only forced courtesy. "I'm sorry, Mr. Summers. We just don't want to give a church first chance on that prime property." He shuffled papers on his desk, looking down at them with a dismissive gesture. That was all. No deal.

Not giving up, I sought and received an appointment with the company president. He was friendlier. He had his company executive board meeting scheduled for early January, 1986 and invited me to come meet the board.

They would consider our project. By now we had a young graphic artist in our church. He created a beautiful display visually depicting what the Prayer Center might look like. We wanted a structure that would architecturally fit into the hill country setting and enhance the overall community development. We would be an asset.

At a friend's Christmas party I made the acquaintance of a seasoned real estate attorney who had done work for the same land developer in both Arizona and New Mexico. He offered to accompany me. The whole church was fasting and praying for this crucial meeting.

In January of 1986 we drove to their impressive high-rise tower in posh Las Colinas office park. The development firm occupied all the eleventh floor, an opulent executive suite, rich in marble and granite. We worked our way through a bevy of secretaries and ended up seated in a leather furnished waiting room. The company board meeting was in progress behind the massive oak doors, we were told. They would call us in to give our presentation.

Finally we were summoned into the room. We shook hands as we were introduced. Pin-stripe suited department heads were all seated around a big conference table.

I spoke cordially and quickly got to the point in respect of their busy day. They listened. I held up our art boards displaying an exhibit of what we planned for the hilltop. We would benefit the present empty neighborhood. We would be a neighborhood center, offering something for all ages. I was through in eight to ten minutes. I was about to open up the floor for questions when the company president asked the sales director what he thought about this.

"We just can't let that hilltop go," Mr. Pearce quickly responded. "It's right in the middle of what we're developing. We need to hold it."

Everyone around the table followed his stand and concurred. The company president thanked us courteously. He expressed his regrets that they had nothing available at the time. He closed his brief remarks with an obligatory hint of future prospects: "But come back in a year or so and see if something might be available that fits your needs."

I had no further presentation. My exit could have been simple and unremarkable. Except that the Spirit bade me to leave them with one short word. My voice was calm and suddenly authoritative.

"Gentlemen," I reminded them, "you vowed in the Dallas City Council Chambers that you would be cooperating with the Christian church in Dallas as you developed your community. If you break your word—then see—let's just see how much property you sell."

Outside the room with the door closed behind us, my attorney friend breathed a big "Whew! Man, I didn't know you would say that." Then he chuckled his approval.

"I certainly never planned it," I responded. "It was not a curse. Nor a threat. It was a simple prediction. Those men *did* give their word to my friend John Evans on the City Council. Now they've reneged on their promise."

"God's still in charge, Robert," my friend counseled. "They can hedge but never head-off the Lord's plan."

As we drove away, we had the distinct feeling that these gentlemen had chosen poorly for the welfare of their company's doing business in Dallas. It did not bode well. It would prove to be a pivotal moment for their future. The word of God is very plain-spoken about this. There is no mincing of words in Proverbs 6:16-17. *There are six things the Lord hates, seven that are detestable to him: haughty eyes, a lying tongue...*

For all the promises of God in Him are Yes, and in Him Amen,
to the glory of God through us.
2 Corinthians 1:20

Truth is so congenial to our mind that we love even the shadow of it.
–Dr. Benjamin Rush, one of the youngest signers of the
Declaration of Independence

Fight when necessary for that which is right
–Texas Rangers' Code

CHAPTER FIVE

DALLAS' HILL COUNTRY

I will lift up my eyes unto the hills—
from whence comes my help?
Psalm 121:1

Texans have an affection for hills that goes back to the days of wide open cattle ranges. The first Anglo settlers were staunch pioneers who avoided the rocky hard-scrabble hills, choosing the better farmlands of the black land prairies. But in the post-Civil War cattle boom, the Texas Hill Country, with its grassy savannahs, became a place of lariat swinging, cattle roping cowboys. They learned from their Mexican counterpart, *the vaquero*, the art of roundups and rodeos. Cattle drives up the Chisholm and Goodnight Trails to Dodge City, Abilene and Fort Sumner (and later Dallas and Fort Worth) became legendary. There the six-shooter and the ten gallon hat were practically standard issue. The cowboy, rounding up strays and driving dusty longhorn herds over purple sage covered rolling hills, would become an icon, a symbol of Texas itself.

The Texas Hill Country tops everyone's list of favorite places in the state. If you want to sell pie to Texans, put a pecan on it. If you aim to sell land to them, call it Hill Country property. Every city slicker and drugstore cowboy will beat a path to your door.

The Hill County with its clear flowing cypress shaded rivers with romantic Spanish names is generally beautiful. Nothing spectacular, but in a wild country sort of way, it is rustic and pleasing. In the springtime it can be enchanting. Texans adore its bluebonnet covered landscapes, especially when the scene is portrayed with an old rock ranch house and the ever present, unique shaped windmill. Texans love it when you expressly throw into the artistic mix the revered longhorns grazing among the wildflowers and cactus. They really like those spotted cows. Ever wonder why?

And by the way, ever wonder where all the millions of heads of longhorn beef originally came from? How'd they get here in Texas? The only plausible explanation is one of history's most intriguing stories of triumph and tragedy. Here's the thumbnail sketch, the digest version.

You have to go way back to the late 1500s to a young, wealthy, Hispanic Jew named Luis de Carvajal. Luis was part of Spain's Sephardic Jewish community. When the Spanish monarchy sought financial aid for its war with the occupying Moors, Luis came to the rescue. Spain succeeded in dispossessing the Moorish invaders. For his help, Luis was given a key appointment in New Spain. After he served as mayor of Tampico, he was deeded by King Felipe (Phillip) a vast territory along the lower Rio Grande (Rio Bravo). Much of this grant was in the region of present day far south Texas. In the early 1590's Luis brought Jewish settlers into his new colony— along with their Andalusian cattle. The story ends in tragedy. The rise of the Spanish Inquisitions brought a cruel dissolution to all legal standing the Jews once had. Along with others, Luis' family was imprisoned for secretly practicing their Jewish faith. They were tortured and burned at the stake. The Inquisitions marked the lowest moment of shame in all Spanish Catholic history.

The cattle of Luis' deserted colonies were abandoned to roam the wilds. The grassy coastal plains were a perfect breeding ground. The herds would multiply until eventually there would be millions of these brown and white dappled longhorns. Two and a half centuries later, the new Republic of Texas (and later the state) had an incredible, unending supply of beef.

After the Civil War, the northern cities of the United States were booming. Their appetite for beef and leather was insatiable. Poor, broke Texans found in their vast supply of cattle a virtual gold mine. Thus began the roundups and cattle drives up the northern trails to the Kansas railheads. From 1867 to 1889 (when the railroads came to Texas) millions of Longhorns were driven north across the Red River by countless cowboys. The cattle drives up the hard tumble trails kept cowboys in their saddles two months at a time. The lore and life of these cattle drovers are the stuff of Western movies. The Old West, the movies remind us, also had bad times and bad guys—the kind of bad guys the Lone Ranger and Roy Rogers faced in weekly television dramas. Cattle rustlers, bank robbers, and hijackers proliferated. Frontier saloons festered with shady characters, four-flushers, cheats, and other miscreants. Evildoers had to be brought to swift justice by gun-toting U.S. Marshals. Yet in this wretched environment, the bold cowboy and the daring frontiersman culture thrived. To this day, the man and his horse remain important to life out in the Hill Country. Ranching is about the only industry out there. The cowboys in those hills are real, not the drug store variety.

And back in big, busy Houston, people still long to live in the hills out west. Every hardhat wearing ship channel laborer would trade his city life for the Western hills—in a heartbeat. The same is true in Dallas. Here our urban cowboys drive the freeways in big, beefy pickups. Alas, as it is said, they are *all hat and no cattle*. They pine for the wide open spaces; for purple sage, rolling hills.

Most everyone, including God Almighty Himself, is fond of hills. Ever notice how many important God appearances take place on the tops of mountains and hills? The Lord reveals Himself to Abraham as Jehovah Jireh on Mount Moriah. Moses encounters God in the burning bush experience at Mount Horeb. God gives the law at Mount Sinai. David sings of God's presence on Mount Zion. He plants his capitol Jerusalem there. Elijah calls down the fire of God on Mount Carmel. Jesus preaches the Sermon on the Mount in Galilee. Later he is transfigured on an exceeding high mountain. Calvary itself is often referenced as Mount Calvary, a place lifted up. In the Hebrew Bible, the verb *'alah* appears more than 800 times. It means to ascend, to go up, to rise. *'Alah* is the root of the word *'aliyah*, "ascension" or "going up" which refers to going up to Zion or returning home to Israel from lands of dispersion.

Hills are a place of solace and strength. So the advertising department of the large development consortium creating the new Villages of Mountain Creek should have had an easy sell with their giant roadside billboards displaying beautiful vistas overlain with the theme, "Dallas' Hill Country." Everything was going their way. You could bet on them, a slam dunk. Location, location, location. They had it all, the only hills around, in a cowboy crazy town known for its boring housing additions built on bald, flatland prairies.

Then how did they manage to squander their winners' luck and end up in financial ruin in thirty months' time? As far-fetched as it seems, their implausible fall began with something so simple as heady, arrogant pride. They just got too big for their britches. They had pledged, in the company of many witnesses, before the Dallas Planning and Zoning board that they would make special plots available to the Christian church in Dallas to purchase. But their early success must have gone to their heads. They began meeting with really big neighborhood developers, Centennial Homes, Crow Development Corporation, KB Homes, Ryland Homes, and so forth. Suddenly they were loath to stoop in order to deal with a small, beginning Christian congregation which dreamed of building a hilltop prayer center. In faith we had already named ourselves Mountain Creek Community Church, planning to locate in that community.

Here's what went wrong with their business plan. The vast 3500 acre ranch they turned into a network of divided parkways, bridges, and intersections was raw range land with absolutely no city utilities. They had to install miles and miles of expensive infrastructure: waterlines, fire hydrants, sanitary sewers, storm water retention ponds, and so forth. Money flowed out of their bank account in every direction like a Texas gusher spewing out of the top of an oil derrick. Second, over in the Middle East, on the other side of the globe, Iran and Iraq were locked in a terrible apocalyptic war. In order to finance this war, both nations sold off millions of barrels of oil at cheap, fire sale prices. Their dumping this glut of crude oil on the world markets drove down the price of West Texas crude to $6.00 per barrel. An unheard of price. Texas oil was now cheaper than bottled drinking water. With the oil price collapse, the state oil business went bust. Like falling dominoes, financial ruin swept across Texas. Banks everywhere began to fail. Savings and Loan Associations, once the prime lender of home mortgages, were devastated. The housing industry was on the ropes, then finally floored. Well known builders and developers went belly up. There was zero market for vacant lots. No one was buying. Not in Houston, San Antonio, or the Dallas/Fort Worth Metroplex. Unfinished, abandoned construction sites littered the urban landscape: even vacant, opulent homes built mostly for doctors, lawyers, and Indian Chiefs with oil wells.

Meanwhile, out in the Villages of Mountain Creek, not one plot of ground sold for a year's time. This I later learned from company insiders. One final blow was that the firm's biggest financial backer, the Power Company of New Mexico (PNM), went into bankruptcy while trying to build one of the largest nuclear reactor power plants in America. Cost overruns chewed up all their cash. PNM was nuked. Flat broke. Out of the picture.

I did not know all of this at the time. I had grown somewhat discouraged waiting for something to break open. We had a great young congregation.

But people were tired of carrying around the portable church equipment in a big white trailer. I was pressured to find a solution—even to look at alternatives. I went to visit a longtime friend, Jim Williams, for advice. He was a lifeline. He had emerged as North Dallas' prime developer of executive class, gated private communities. A very savvy civic voice, he was chairman of the Cotton Bowl Committee which sponsored New Year's Day college bowl games in Dallas. He had survived the real estate bust, barely. I needed a good brother's assurance. My faith was flagging.

"Jim," I asked, "With all that's happened should I give up on the hill and try to locate the ministry somewhere else?"

His counsel was typical Jim—right to the point. "Robert," he responded with a voice loaded with firmness, "what did God say to you?" He pinned me. "Stick to your dream! Don't settle for anything less."

I felt rebuked for my faltering trust in God's best. But Jim was right. And I knew it. Nonetheless, I did manage to look at one more alternative site that someone in our circle of friends really wanted me to survey. This time the rebuke I received was not from a man. While walking over this property, I felt the distinct correcting presence of the Holy Spirit. "What are you doing out here?" The Spirit Himself clearly spoke to my spirit. I knew it was the Lord. I was undone. I retreated to my car. I had no answer and was weary of running here and there.

I went home and told JoAn about the Spirit's guidance. We asked the Lord to forgive my unbelief and help my faith. An hour later the phone rang. JoAn answered. "Yes, he's here. Hold on, I'll get him for you," she replied to the man on the other end of the line who asked to speak to "a Pastor Summers."

I took the phone. The man sounded relieved. He explained he had been trying to contact me for the last hour or so. He introduced himself as Bill Boyajan, the new marketing director for the Mountain Creek developers. The company president had told him his first assignment was to "Find that preacher!" Then he offered, "Can I take you to breakfast in the morning?"

Breakfast was a pleasant experience with this sharp, friendly, well-dressed young man. He showed me all the respect of a fellow Christian. He told me the company now wanted to make that hilltop tract available to our church. He was authorized *to bring us to the table* if we would just make an offer on the land. The company would entertain any good faith, reasonable offer. He encouraged me. I left that conversation amazed and happy. It was obvious that we now had the advantage. I knew this was God's doing.

Back at our church office, I fished out the business card of Al Block, the former vice president of the community development corporation. He had left the developer to form his own consultant business. Al is the man who arranged the helicopter flyover so he could personally show me the mountain. He seemed to be expecting my call. He listened to my report of the breakfast meeting with the new marketing director.

"Don't offer them a penny more than what they paid for that land," he was quick to reply. "Pastor Summers, they haven't sold one tract of property in the last twelve months. They are in a terrible bind. They need you more than you need them. And I mean it." Wow. That last statement stunned me.

Al continued. "Here's what they paid for that raw land. Twenty-seven thousand an acre. You offer them that figure and they'll sign that land over to your church. Make them carry the note. You're in a good position, Robert," he stated firmly. "Deal tough with them. Call me if you need help."

I was flat out surprised and blessed by Al Block's coaching and savvy. JoAn and I knew this was a God moment. We were going to win this one. We gave Him all the glory.

We sat down and began composing this letter, stating our final offer. The next day, July 4, 1986, the church staff assembled to pray over our letter. That day is still quite clear in my memory. A big hometown parade had formed near our offices. In the distance I could hear the rousing victory notes of Bagley's *National Emblem* march. The dream of Prayer Mountain was coming true. The Lord's people were going out to take possession of the highest point in Dallas. And the whole town seemed to be celebrating this victory with us.

Now it happened just as Mr. Al Block had predicted. Three days later we received a telephone call from Bill Boyajan informing us that our offer had been accepted. The next day we were sitting down with the new marketing director drawing up papers of agreement on Tract 24B as the mountain was described in the company's original master plan.

The whole project was still in the process of being surveyed and platted. Although our site was unmistakable, there was no legal metes and bounds description of it. Any contract for deed would need that information for the official record.

When the survey crew came out they could find no nearby reference points (Global Positioning Satellite technology was still a few years away). They finally located an old U.S. Geological Survey bench marker monumented in a great rock on a hilltop a mile away. Our present survey is referenced back to that big rock, which now is part of the Dallas Cedar Ridge Nature Preserve, managed by the Audubon Society.

Like the survey team, we still look *back to the Rock who begot us.* When we signed the papers, closing the deal on the hilltop, seventeen years had come and gone since the Lord had first shown me a glimpse of the mountain. (The time I had viewed it through the airplane window.) The little boy who had suffered a broken leg was now a young man. Kip graduated in 1986 from a large nearby high school and left the same summer on a short term mission to Moscow, Russia. Selah! Who could have known this seventeen years ago?

Is there a plausible explanation for the ways of the Lord? Certainly. It is a no-brainer for people of faith. In Romans 10:17 the Apostle, writing by the Spirit, declares, "Faith comes by hearing, and hearing by the Word of God." The expression *Word of God* in its Greek original form is the word *rhema,* meaning an utterance, or something said. When the Lord uttered that word, saying to my spirit, *What a great place to build a prayer center for Dallas,* it was a seed dropped into the soil of my soul. It took root and sprang up as a vision. Now seventeen years later, the seed had become a healthy tree planted by living waters. It would bring forth its fruit in its season.

The farmer, when he plants, does not merely see seed. He sees beyond. And he thinks beyond to a season of harvest. We need that kind of vision. This is all the Lord asks when He assures us: *So shall My word be that goes forth from My mouth; It shall not return to Me void, But it shall accomplish what I please, And it shall prosper in the thing for which I sent it.*[8]

Jack W. Hayford, in commenting on that particular verse writes, "All increase of life within His love comes by His Word, as human response gives place for His blessing. When received, God's word of promise will never be barren. The power in His Word will always fulfill the promise of His Word."[9]

The record will show that from the beginning we have recognized that this high place is God's hill. We are mere stewards and caretakers of it. The future destiny of this hilltop is determined by the Lord alone.

For the Lord is the great God
And the great King above all gods.
In His hand are the deep places of the earth;
The heights of the hills are His also
The sea is His, for He made it;
And His hands formed the dry land.
Oh come, let us worship and bow down;
Let us kneel before the Lord our Maker
For He is our God,
And we are the people of His pasture
And the sheep of His hand.
Psalm 95:3-7

If a man believes in unalterable natural law,
he cannot believe in any miracle in any age.
If a man believes in a will behind law,
he can believe in any miracle in any age.
–G.K. Chesterton, Orthodoxy

CHAPTER SIX

WHAT DO THESE STONES MEAN?

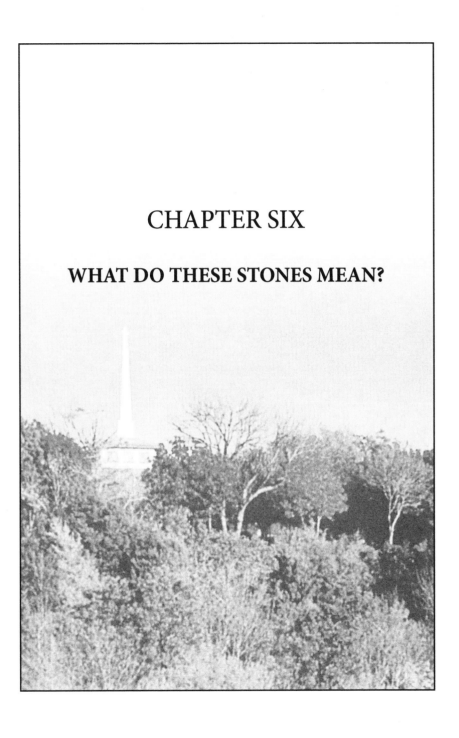

These stones shall be for a memorial to the children of Israel forever.
Joshua 4:7

You will arise and have mercy on Zion;
for the time to favor her,
yes, the set time has come.
For Your servants take pleasure in her stones,
and show favor to her dust.
Psalm 102:13,14

Lord God of Hosts be with us yet, Lest we forget, lest we forget.
from *Recessional* by Rudyard Kipling

Charlie Rodgers hung onto every word I told him about the Lord. He would have me tell him the gospel over and over. I baptized him in Canyon Lake in the summer of '79. He was the very last of the Jesus Movement wave that came rolling into our Church in the Wildwood.

Charlie was not actually a Jesus Person, not by a long shot. He had never smoked dope. He had certainly never been a hippie. He wore wrinkle-free polyester trousers. He was a veteran of World War II front lines in Europe. So he was not young. But he loved the young disciples and our church's youthful worship. He had experienced such a great healing, he was free and absolutely enthusiastic about every service we held. His zeal for the church and for the service of the Kingdom was unexcelled. His enthusiasm and commitment would follow us to Dallas and play a key role in the design of our new Prayer Center.

When we moved to Dallas, Charlie packed up and moved away from Canyon Lake. He went further west out into the wide open ranching region of Bandera County in the Hill Country. Charlie was an expert in rock quarrying. He had managed large scale quarries producing building stone, the basic material for architectural construction in Southwest Texas. Charlie developed a small quarry of his own out in the middle of nowhere. Because he was such a private person, he told us little about it.

We went to visit him when he fell ill with cancer. He was bedridden in his big mobile home that was set up near a clear blue Hill Country lake.

That is when he told me about his quarry. He drew me a sketchy diagram of where the best rock was located. He had paid his workers to cut and stack it up ready for loading and shipping.

"Use this rock to build your prayer center in Dallas," he charged me with a voice weak and tired. "I quarried it for you to have. I've talked to several truckers about hauling it. One tried to buy it. Another, I think, tried to steal the rock. It's the best rock I could find. It has a golden cast to it—like Jerusalem stone. It has a monument quality to it."

"Charlie," I replied in surprise, "you didn't tell me you were doing this."

"I never told anyone." He coughed but managed a smile. "Use this and build something beautiful on that mountain. I wanted rock that looked like Jerusalem stone. I'm giving this as a memorial."

"A memorial for what?" I puzzled.

"Remember when I showed you all those Army photographs taken in Germany when we liberated that death camp?" he asked. "Before I die I want to do something good as a memorial, some kind of remembrance for all those tortured souls. No one can believe how cruel the Nazis were. I'll never forget what I witnessed there. How could I?" he concluded with a grimace of deep regret.

I too could not forget that moment, now seven years ago, when Charlie began to pour out his heart with all its suppressed anguish and pain. It was obvious he had struggled emotionally under the disgusting pall of that spectacle and its lingering aftermath. The grim horrors of the War had stunted his youthful optimism. It had marked him. Although in these last seven years his mind had slowly healed, thanks to prayer and daily Bible reading.

At that time Charlie was a new friend. He was helping me restore my relic of a pickup. JoAn referred to my 1969 Ford Econoline as my *Tonka truck*. It had a bright new paint job, but its old engine was shot. Exchanging an engine in this truck was a monster project because of its cab over the motor configuration. Charlie had built a tall ramp. We parked the truck up on the ramp so we could pull the engine out the bottom side.

Charlie was a great mechanic, really good. But he was terribly nervous. He was a shaky, chain smoker. He could maintain his concentration no more than thirty to forty minutes at a time. He sweated his polyester clothing profusely. He smelled like an old man, full of years.

What Do these Stones Mean?

We had just stepped inside his trailer house for a coffee break when I broached the subject. "Charlie, you're a nervous wreck," I exclaimed in my most caring pastoral voice. "What's wrong? You are a wounded soul. I want to help you."

Fidgeting to light another cigarette between his shaky fingers, he responded, "I didn't know it showed. I guess it does." He continued after a short pause to look away and take a deep breath. "Yeah, I guess it does," he sighed. "Wish I could find the answer. God knows I've tried."

I looked into his sad cocker spaniel eyes. His skinny leather face was a sea of twitches and tics. Hardened worry lines dug furrows into his every expression. Topping off his eroded looks was the faint remnant of a once proud wave in his thinning hair. The man's shiny scalp now shone through randomly. Charlie was careworn and too soon old. If anyone needed God's peace, Charlie did. Desperately. He needed a new heart and a new mind. Like my old pickup, he needed a whole new engine, not just a tune up. Healing this old wounded soldier would be a real project.

This was the day Charlie asked the Lord for a new heart. He admitted this was the first time in years he had wept. Today his tears were for joy and relief. Soon he began telling me about his past, including his wartime encounter at an atrocious death camp. He hauled down a lockbox from up in his closet. Loaded with his World War II service memorabilia, the box was like a secret time machine—and Charlie was sharing it with me. Since Charlie was not a foot soldier, he was not highly decorated. But he had saved scores of photographs, editions of *Stars and Stripes* the military journal, as well as letters and written notes. He began to take me down memory lane. I could tell by the tone of his voice that Charlie's war memory throbbed with pain.

Charlie was a tank repair mechanic attached to 101st Cavalry Group (Mechanized). Battling through France and entering Germany in the winter of '44-'45, General Patton's 3rd Army tanks were constantly on the move through ice and snow. Charlie's job was to scout out large buildings and warehouses where the big fighting machines could be pulled in out of the bitter cold weather for needed repairs.

Early Sunday morning, April 29th, the 101st Cavalry led a task force from the 157th Infantry into a small town in southern Germany. Charlie followed along in his tool-laden heavy duty jeep, searching the skyline for a big building he could expropriate as a temporary service garage. Just as he was headed toward a large structure and smokestack on the other side of the town center, his walkie-talkie crackled with a report. It was a buddy of his, a tanker captain whose tank Charlie kept in fine tune. "Charlie! Come in! You there?" the excited voice called. "Man, Charlie, we've just blasted a fleeing Nazi transport full of groceries. Lots of sardines. You interested?"

"Canned sardines!" responded Charlie. He began salivating as if he could already taste his favorite dish. He had really missed real food. Sick of C-ration field lunches, he had written home at Christmas and told how he was dreaming about sardines. He ended his letters with a usual P.S.S. which stood for *please send sardines*. None came. At least none managed to reach him out on the blood and guts battlefront in Patton's 3rd Army's swift push into Germany.

"Tell me where you are. I'm on my way," exclaimed Charlie. He hastened down the artillery shell-pocked road. The loud booms of big guns had now moved away into the distance. Coming alongside the smoldering ruin of a heavy truck surrounded by GI's, Charlie loaded his jeep as high as possible with crate upon crate of canned sardines. This was a dream come true.

As he turned his loaded jeep back toward town, he headed it toward those large structures he had decided to inspect. He approached some kind of high fenced compound which he first thought to be a secure munitions depot. He found the gate heavily chained and padlocked. As he was pulling out his bolt cutters to cut it open, a U.S. Army medic arrived with two well-armed infantry men. The medic explained that his company was already entering the gates on the far side, dislodging any armed opposition. He had just received information that there were many prisoners held here who were dying of starvation.

As Charlie cut open the gate, the medic was already thinking ahead. "Soldier, can you take your jeep and get us some food? Do you know where we might find something to feed these dying souls?"

Charlie turned the medic around to look at his sardine laden jeep. "Sure do!" Charlie shot back. "Just look at all those sardines. That's maybe a thousand cans of sardines, more or less!'

"Sardines! God, that's perfect," uttered the medic as he helped Charlie push open the big gate. "That's absolutely perfect. Let's get moving."

They cut their way through more gates, just in time to meet up with some of the men of Company I of the 157th near what was marked as a hospital building. These soldiers were busy rounding up German soldiers who appeared to be SS Guards. Sporadic small arms fire still sounded from around the corner.

Proceeding toward the center of the compound, Charlie's group suddenly happened upon a big, ugly, barbed-wire confining fence surrounded by a deep, moat-like concrete ditch. Dead bodies lay in the ditch. The liberators had unknowingly stumbled into a horrible concentration camp called Dachau. Looming before their eyes was the unbelievable sight: Thousands upon thousands of gaunt, skeletal, prison-garbed people, barely human in appearance were pressed up against the fence. Their ear-splitting cacophony of wails and cries for help grew louder as more and more prisoners poured out of the barracks to join in the tumult. The horror-filled faces of this tortured multitude was worse than a thousand nightmares. Charlie felt a fluid and fearful sickness sweep over him. Everywhere he glanced, Dachau was unbelievable rot and filth mingled with the vile stench of death.

Brigadier Gen. Felix Sparks would report that day that his battle-hardened veterans of six major campaigns became sickened and vomited. His logged entry states that they "became extremely distraught. Some cried, while others raged. Some thirty minutes passed before I could restore order and discipline."[10] Then Lieutenant Colonel Sparks would never forget that day. Neither would Charlie. Never!

The chilling carnage—all the unburied and decaying dead, untold thousands, was absolutely beyond imagination. Lieutenant Colonel Sparks dispatched military police teams with jeep mounted public-address loudspeakers to order out all the Dachau citizens to meet in the city square and prepare for the burial of the dead.

Meanwhile, U.S. soldiers were now busy assisting the medics in a stopgap feeding program until more food arrived. Each starving prisoner was given the ration of a heaping spoonful of sardines. Emaciated and starving, they filed by like dead men barely walking. Untold thousands of grim-faced, frail-bodied prisoners were yet lined in an orderly manner. Most were Jews. They were conspicuously marked by the yellow Star of David on their threadbare prison garb. Charlie later learned the count—about 30,000 in all. Miraculously, the sardine supply held out until all were fed a bite. The unrelenting, gnawing torture of hunger was now over, at least for the living.

The Seventh Army came in the next day and took over the camp's administration. With them came truckloads of food, medical supplies, and bedding. April 30th, according to Charlie's Army news clippings, the citizens of Dachau township were commanded to dress up in their best and report with shovels for the mandatory burying of the dead. The U.S. colonels insisted the town's people provide the bodies with a modicum of funeral dignity. There would be no more bulldozed trench pits for the dead at Dachau—even though the process by hand would go on for days.

Charlie, ever graced with the gift of fading into anonymity, pulled out with the 101st heading southeast for Rosenheim and the Autobahn toward Berchtesgaden. His team bounced along in his heavy-duty jeep, continuing their artful fix and repair jobs for Patton's Third Army. The general's brilliant campaign, rushing headlong ablaze with firepower, blasted through roadblock after roadblock. The army of the Third Reich, Hitler's dread Wehrmacht, was everywhere a crumbling, retreating remnant. Patton's army brigades were in hot pursuit. They made swift dispatch of the defenses at every roadblock. Marching on, they turned eastward through Traunstein, Salzburg, and on east to Linz and Vienna, Austria. The God of Israel had loosed the fateful lightning of His terrible swift sword. As it is written:

He who avenges blood remembers; He does not ignore the cry of the afflicted.[11]

The war ended with Charlie in Vienna. The occasion provided him one pleasant memory. Charlie loved horses. Patton also loved horses. So he ordered the arena and stables where Vienna's prized Lipizzaner stallions were quartered to be spared. Perhaps that was the cowboy in Patton. We'll never know, for Patton himself died in a car wreck only weeks after the war ended. Having told me all these things, Charlie seemed to be at an end to a much needed catharsis. He had delivered his soul.

Our last visit with Charlie was another treasured walk down memory lane. JoAn and I knew it was God-ordained. Charlie was now in his late sixties and dying of cancer. He told me that he wanted me to minister his memorial service. This shrunken and pain-wracked hero could easily have been written into Hebrews 11 among those who are listed at the last as unnamed; only mentioned as "others." Unnamed, but not unknown to God.

Charlie passed less than a month after our bedside visit. His memorial service was held in his hometown of Kerrville, Texas. In my remarks I used Psalm 87:6 as a theme, where it says of Zion, "This one was born there," and "All my wellsprings are in you." (verse 7) I related the episode of how Charlie had come face to face with unimaginable evil at Dachau. Yet Charlie's life testified of grace and deliverance from evil. He found hope in Jesus Christ. Although he never discounted the horror of the Holocaust, he came to see his one black day at the death camp as divinely ordained. For one brief moment, Charlie was cast into the role of Angel of Mercy. And he was perfect in that role. He was a natural, for never did he assume the air and appearance of a hero.

We were surprised at how many of his old friends turned out for his funeral. But only a handful of his acquaintances knew about his World War II experiences. His childhood friends had called him "Mutt" all his life. They were stunned to hear that dear ole nervous Mutt had lived his last seven years at peace with God. Their puzzled glances and gestures to one another as I spoke were in a sense the highlight of the service.

A sun wrinkled, sad faced old cowboy, dressed up in his best, hard worn Western polyester suit peered into Charlie's casket. He gripped my hand with his own leathery hand. He offered me a soft, tearful "thanks." Glancing back at Charlie's still, peaceful countenance, he spoke in a low voice, "Charlie, you was a good man." He wiped his tears with his sleeve and hastened out to conceal his weeping. "A very good man," he mumbled.

We buried Charlie's remains by the clear flowing Guadalupe, his favorite river. This enigmatic friend of ours had long ago purchased his own burial plot in Nichols Cemetery within a stone's throw of the Hill Country waters. A surprise to the very end.

I remembered how Charlie, from his bedfast position, had strictly warned us in his best secret agent fashion, "Don't dare leave that rock lying out there unattended. It's beautiful stone. Someone will haul it off for sure." Charlie had done some kind of work for the CIA but remained close-mouthed about any details. So as soon as I could return to the Hill Country village of Bandera, near Charlie's quarry, I sought for a hauler. I asked around the town and its small courthouse square. The leathery old cowboys who hung around the courthouse were friendly, but no one knew anybody with a rock hauling rig. Finally in a café, the manager told me he had already heard talk of the fresh quarried rock out there at Charlie's place. He knew the name of a man, Charles Cade, over in Comfort who had a quarry and a big rock hauling truck. In the yellow page phonebook, I noticed this man had a fish logo in his business advertisement. I called him. He was friendly and understanding.

"You called me last week, didn't you?" Mr. Cade asked.

Surprised, I responded, "No, not me."

Immediately he came back, "Well, it was you, or else someone in your group. Some man called me up wanting to ask about hauling a hundred tons of stone up to a hilltop in Dallas—to build a chapel." He had a Wilford Brimley mellow voice.

Really, I was stunned. We all were. We couldn't imagine how anyone else in the world knew this much about our plans to get that rock up to Dallas. Charlie Rodgers had been dead and buried for several weeks.

"Charlie's angel," JoAn explained. Her way of solving the puzzle brought a chuckle from all of us. But none of us could come up with a plausible answer as to who had placed that call to Mr. Cade.

A half dozen or more of our church men went to Charlie's little ranch to help Mr. Cade load up our first big shipment. A friend even came over from Canyon Lake with a lumber truck to help us haul away the stone. When we stopped in Marble Falls for a much deserved lunch, we were approached by a builder who offered to buy our stone. Back at the hill in Dallas we were so thrilled with our big pile of rocks. We had a treasure. Our project was proceeding. But obviously we were not doing it the usual way. We had rock, tons of rock. But we had no building plan yet. We needed an architect. The rock we had was, in a sense, hallowed. Solid rock. The Lord's rock: memorial stone. Given unto the Lord.

What Do these Stones Mean?

Every breakthrough brought us a joyous sense of gratitude and expectation. And to this very day we have never solved the big mystery. The Lord alone knows who called Charles Cade about that "rock to be hauled up to a hilltop in Dallas, for a chapel." God alone knows. However, I was not overly surprised, knowing my friend Charlie. He lived by the motto found on the crest and shield of the 101st Cav: *TO THE UTMOST.*

Whenever we look at the beautiful stone on the chapel we remember Charlie as one of the last of the Greatest Generation. He was one of those great Americans who overcame the Great Depression and then fought and won the World War. He was always ready to give his all. America will miss his generation.

Here the inmates were underfed, worked into living skeletons, and stacked on shelves for their five hours' sleep a night. Disease ran wild. Prisoners were tortured, driven insane, beaten, and degraded, and every known atrocity conceived by man was committed.
–Leon Uris, *Exodus*, Doubleday, New York, p. 146

In the early dawn wraith-like figures could be seen wandering aimlessly along the roads and through the fields. They turned out to be hollow-eyed, living skeletons wearing striped pajama-like garments hanging from their protruding bones. Up ahead heavy, dark smoke arose above a tree line and behind it we came upon one of Hitler's notorious concentration camps. Inside was pure horror. –Colonel Charles K. Graydon from his *World War II memoirs of the 101st Cavalry (Mechanized)*.

If the Mountain Could Speak

For He looked down from the height of His sanctuary;
From heaven the Lord viewed the earth,
To hear the groaning of the prisoner,
To release those appointed to death,
To declare the name of the Lord in Zion,
And His praise in Jerusalem.
Psalm 102:19-21

He upholds the cause of the oppressed
And gives food to the hungry.
The Lord sets prisoners free.
Psalm 146:7 NIV

The Lord builds up Jerusalem: He gathers the exiles of Israel.
He heals the brokenhearted and binds up their wounds.
Psalm 147:2,3 NIV

Blessed are the merciful,
for they shall obtain mercy.
–Jesus in Matthew 5:7

CHAPTER SEVEN

THEY STOLE OUR CROSS

But God forbid that I should boast except in the cross of our Lord Jesus Christ, by whom the world has been crucified to me, and I to the world.
Galatians 6:14

In our early days the mountain was such a rough and inaccessible place that few people would hazard a visit. Very few did come. The exception was the uninvited four-wheelers, those with big, macho four wheel drive trucks. And those who came out secretly at night, the witches.

Our first few attempts to make the summit a peaceful place for prayer met with destruction or at least mischief and vandalism. They stole all our park benches and tables. To put a stop to this traffic, we installed large iron gates at both ends of the lane which ran through the property. We continued to pray and cleanse the property by declaring the Word of the Lord over it. One of our carpenters made a large, old rugged cross and erected it at the top of the road. Quite soon, a dead black cat was tied by its tail to our front gate. Curses and threats were etched into the rocky shale drive below the gate. A huge pentagram was also drawn into the lane.

Then it happened.

"They stole our cross!" the young men of the church exclaimed when I came out to bring cold water to the work crew atop the hill. The cross was indeed missing from its place. It had been lifted up, installed in the only opening where there was an unobstructed view through the trees to the valley below. The picturesque site was just across the road from where we had earlier found a charred stone altar.

When word of this theft spread through our congregation, Jerry, our praise leader vowed to pray conviction on the thieves. I thought he was typically over-optimistic. Maybe it would be best to simply put up another cross. But Jerry wanted them to bring back the old one. He prompted all of us to pray about it.

Months passed. No cross appeared. I had come to accept it, that is the heist of the cross. Who knows what kind of jerk would rip off a big old rugged cross?

The following spring I drove out in my pickup to take sandwiches to my son Kipling, who was now in college, and another stout young man.

They were clearing the thickets of briar and brush atop the hill. Just as I rounded the first bend coming up the lane, I saw it. Immediately the hand of the Lord seemed to halt me in the road. Up the hill a graphic scene, or should I say spectacle, was being portrayed. This was a depiction, a human video of a classic photograph. Two young men were struggling to lift a heavy wooden cross into its place. Our old rugged cross! For a few seconds their lifting and heaving created a picture, a dead ringer rendering, of the famous World War II Rosenthal photograph of the U.S. Marines lifting Old Glory at the summit of Mount Suribachi on Iwo Jima. Quite a show. And they never saw me. It was a scene caught in the Kodak of my soul, saved on the iPad of my heart.

Instantly the Lord spoke to my spirit, *Your stolen cross was returned because I issued a mandate that it must be brought back. Just as your cross was taken away, the message of My cross has been taken away from My church. I am mandating that it must be returned. Some will rediscover it, many of them little known, will find it and raise it up again. My favor will rest upon those who do.*

I was undone. I wept. Personally I had few sermons on the cross—mainly for communion times. Believe me, I was in that instant experiencing a major paradigm shift. Only when the young men finished erecting the cross did I drive on up. They seemed oblivious to the fact that they had provided me such a spectacle. They had found the old cross leaning up against our back gate where it had been returned. They had carried the cross back to its original station. There they lifted it up.

My message priority shift continued. JoAn and I were traveling, a short time later in northern France. We were visiting with some of our European missionary families. We took an extra few days in Normandy and Brittany. We drove out to tour Mont Ste. Michelle. The drive was more a circuit through French farmlands. Caught in the string of traffic backed up behind French farmers pulling hay wagons with their tractors was as frustrating as the constant showers which pelted our little Renault.

We finally arrived late afternoon at Le Petite QuinQuin, our village B and B. We were only five kilometers from Ste. Michelle. Our bedroom balcony had a clear view of the famed distant mountain with its signature abbey and spire protruding heavenward. I was worn out from driving. But the skies were now clear.

JoAn eagerly wanted to proceed and visit the shrine. I suggested we would rest up and go out in the morning. But I gave in to her insistence. I was glad I did. That was one of the most rewarding late afternoons I have ever spent. The unfolding views of Mont Ste. Michelle from a distance were breathtaking. But only when you actually enter across the causeway into the village do you begin to see its hundreds of sites and amazing details. In all its holy places you will find throngs of pilgrims. Then there are the many tourists searching through curious and intriguing little shops, buying everything from novelties to an occasional *objet d'art*. The wonder of Mont Ste. Michelle was that every square inch is rich in history. There was not one bland foot of ground in the place. French speaking children frolicked in its narrow streets. Its winding, steep lane led us through ancient cemeteries, older than our nation. At every turn the view of the deep blue La Manche, or the English Channel, was exhilarating. The mountain rises above a spit of land which juts out into the sea.

Finally, the abbey at the top is truly one of the world's wonders. Perched atop this three hundred foot rocky peak, its spire rises another hundred and twenty feet upward. The ancient church has a rich and storied past. Its structure dates back to the ancient time of the Normans. JoAn and I love architecture and ancient cathedrals. (Two days later we visited the Cathedral of Chartres with its flying buttresses.) But this ambitious achievement was built entirely without modern machinery. It was constructed by committed holy men with great and patient vision. Their project would cover many generations—even hundreds of years.

I came away from Mont Ste. Michelle with my new paradigm of the cross further expanded. The cross is like that distant mountain in many Christians' view. Its shape is like a small icon—far away on their visual horizon. Perhaps it is a distinct silhouette, or some miniature configuration far off from their daily affairs. It remains far too distant to be appreciated for what it is. Only when the forces of destiny crowd them up close to the cross do they discover that there is so much more here than meets the eye. Faith *cometh* only when we are close to the cross of Christ. Too much which passes for gospel in our times bears little resemblance to the message of the cross.

When I speak of the cross I am talking about the core message of the gospel: salvation through the sacrifice of the Lamb of God at Calvary. This is what the Apostle Paul declared to be of the *first* order of importance:

For what I received I passed on to you as of first importance: that Christ died for our sins according to the Scriptures, that he was buried, that he was raised on the third day according to the Scriptures, and that he appeared to Peter, and then the Twelve. After that, he appeared to more than five hundred of the brothers at the same time.[12] Paul goes on to say *last of all he appeared to me also.*[13] Paul held that the message of the cross was central to the New Testament just as the Passover was central to the Old. Christ was the fulfillment of Passover, he instructs: *For Christ, our Passover lamb, has been sacrificed. Therefore let us keep the Festival...*[14]

I believe that if the Apostle had a business card or a website it would say, *We preach Christ crucified...*

When I began to study and preach about the cross, I found that I was preaching out some members who refused to believe, and preaching in those who heard the call to follow Christ. Our congregation began to change for the better. We went from being hesitant in battle to being resolute. We found that, like Gideon, we could accomplish more with less—as long as we had agreement. We could by grace enjoy real victories as long as we stayed humbly on our knees.

The great divine irony is this: only God could turn the cross into a symbol of hope. The Roman cross was the be-all and end-all form of cruel and unusual punishment meant to utterly devastate. It is truly amazing grace that God turns it for good. When vandals stole our cross, they began an episode of faith for us. Little did they know *that all things work together for good for those who love God and are called according to His purposes.*[15] Not all things are good. But they do work for our good.

And our old rugged cross still staunchly stands in the very spot where my son Kipling raised it up again those many years ago. Our hilltop is marked today by a much larger, lighted cross—a symbol of hope. But the old one, like Jeremiah's "old path" remains my favorite. It reminds me of the rude cross that Jesus died upon to save me from my sins. My dear, late dad loved books on the cross of Christ. He framed a favorite statement in barn board and barbed wire penned by Britain's Major Ian Thomas:

"I simply argue that the cross be raised again at the center of the market place as well as on the steeple of the church. I am recovering the claim that Jesus was not crucified in a cathedral between two candles but on a cross between two thieves; on the town garbage heap; at a crossroads so cosmopolitan that they had to write His title in Hebrew and in Latin and in Greek…at the kind of place where cynics talk smut, and thieves curse, and soldiers gamble. Because that is where he died and that is what he died about. And that is where churchmen ought to be and what churchmen should be about."

That rough framed statement was posted for every student at Wildwood School to observe as they entered for worship. They still remember the effect of those words.

For I am not ashamed of the gospel of Christ, for it is the power of God to
salvation for everyone who believes, for the Jew first and also for the Greek.
For in it the righteousness of God is revealed from faith to faith;
as it is written, 'The just shall live by faith.'
–Paul in Romans 1:16-17

Carry the cross patiently, and with perfect submission;
and in the end it shall carry you.
–Thomas a Kempis, *Of the Imitation of Christ*

All true theology must be developed within earshot
of the cry of the cross of Christ.
–An old English church adage.

CHAPTER EIGHT

HOW BEAUTIFUL ON THE MOUNTAINS

How beautiful upon the mountains
Are the feet of him who brings good news,
Who proclaims peace
Who brings glad tidings of good things
Who proclaims salvation
Who says to Zion,
"Your God reigns."
Isaiah 52:7

You also, as living stones, are being built up a spiritual house, a holy priesthood...
1 Peter 2:5

Of all fond memories about Prayer Mountain, star billing goes to the wonderful people who helped bring this vision to life. We thank our God every time we remember them. We could not have done this by ourselves. Nor would we have wanted to. Like the challenge of young Titus sent by Paul to do a work in Crete, this assignment was often difficult, dirty, and discouraging. God sent us people, living stones, that we could lean on, we could count on. They stood tough for the cause of Christ. God made them "iron pillars" in the words of Jeremiah 1:18. They were chosen instruments. The force of the church moves not with numbers, but with loyal, serving saints.

In the midst of the dark night of the soul, their coming brought us sunny moments of breakthrough. Nothing dazzling. Just clear-headed help and encouragement. Practical get-the-job-done help. They were truly praying people. Only praying people understand and seek the Lord for miracles and divine intervention. How can we say thanks to all of them?

It is certainly the challenge of any frontlines ministry to find positive people like Caleb and Joshua, whom the Word describes as being of "a different spirit." They are committed to the good report. It is a given fact of our Christian faith that we can see more accomplished through a smaller number of true believers than with a big mixed multitude which has wobbly faith. That is the lesson of the famous Gideon's *Three Hundred*. Every vision requires faithful people who are fearless in the face of giants and bad odds.

J.D. and Martha Dowd fit into this last category. In the spring of '88 I called J.D. for help. He had been my favorite Sunday School teacher in Houston when I was in his Junior Boy's class over thirty years previous. He was a heavy equipment operator, now retired. He had sold off his business. We needed a waterline installed, I told him.

J.D. chuckled in his trademark joking style. "Martha and I are ready to leave Houston and hit the road," he told me enthusiastically. He went on to tell me it was now their desire to go places to assist ministries in new construction. They had a large motor home. "Rent me a John Deere 210C backhoe, Robert," he encouraged. "We'll come on up there and get that waterline in." He was confident. And I needed some confidence at that point.

The City of Dallas, especially the Dallas Fire Department, required us to install a four inch waterline to supply our private line fire hydrant. Also down at the street level, they needed a city Fire Department hydrant installed on the city water main. To boost our private waterline, we would need to engineer and encase fire department connections at street level. This connection included a complex of valves in a concrete ground vault. The valves would allow fire department pumper trucks to power up the pressure in our private line without a high pressure backflow discharging into the city water main.

The line we were installing had a rise of 120 feet in elevation from the city street to our building site. The line itself was over 1200 feet in length. All of this was no small project, involving several engineered drawings, City Hall bonded utility contractors, and scores of permits.

We could have become discouraged had it not been for J.D. and Martha's sunny demeanor. Here's one very interesting example, one of many.

The Dallas Fire Department code required all waterlines which supply fire sprinklers and such to be buried three feet below the ground surface. They must be packed in red cushioning sand. The trench J.D. dug running up the mountain involved six days of digging. He had to stop twice to repair the backhoe's rock bucket because the hard shale rock on the mountain busted its steel teeth. Several young men of the church volunteered to help clean and prep the ditch, as well as smooth and pack the select fill cushion sand. Finally we were ready for the water pipe.

Mack Gray, a long time irrigation supply man in our congregation, had ordered the pipe at a real cost savings. Our plumber utilized the young volunteers to help him install the 1200 feet of Schedule 40 "Blue Brute" PVC water pipe. We called for an inspection, eager to bury the trench. We had to hurry. Severe thunderstorms were forecast to roll into Dallas. Our trench was open and vulnerable.

The city inspector came out. He appeared agitated. After taking a cursory look, he immediately shut down our project with his red tag "Stop" order. He flatly stated that we were installing the wrong PVC pipe. The exact schedule numbers on the pipe were unfamiliar to him. We protested that we had already cleared these numbers with the Plumbing Department at City Hall. He refused to listen. He just walked away, scooted into his little white official city automobile, and drove down off the hill.

Before I could get back downtown to appeal this decision to his supervisor, City Hall closed for the day. That same night bad weather developed right over Dallas. We got a big gully washer four inch rain on the mountain. When we arrived at the job site the next morning we found our waterline ditch had become a swift current creek, a cascade carrying water and sand downhill, dumping it out on the street below. Almost all seventy yards of select fill sand now covered the city street at the bottom of the hill turning it sandy red.

Down at City Hall I had an appointment with the chief plumbing inspector. He carefully inspected a piece of our pipe, thoroughly checking over its printed schedule numbers.

"This pipe's good," he concluded. "More than meets code. The numbers on it are printed out a bit differently. That's what you get when you order through a company other than a plumbing supply." He pulled out a green "Proceed" tag from his desk, signed it, and pushed it over to me. "Sorry about the problem," he apologized.

As I drove back to the hill, I was ticked. Really ticked. I found J.D. working with the John Deere tractor smoothing down our roadway. I wanted him to help me stay mad at Dallas City Plumbing. Instead, he told me a long ol' story about an inspector in Houston back in the 1970's who made him redo a storm sewer manhole. When he finally wrapped up the moral of his story, he had me feeling sorry for that city guy. Then we prayed about the waterline and our relationship with City Hall. I felt better. Much better. It just wasn't worth animosity toward the Big D city officials. Thankfully, J.D. was able to recover much of the lost sand with the big bucket loader. That afternoon the little official white Plymouth marked Plumbing Inspector, City of Dallas came putt-putting up the hill with our friend from City Hall. The visit was short and sweet. Just long enough for him to tell us, "Go ahead. Bury the line."

That was not our friend's last visit. Many plumbing inspections later, he showed up with tears in his eyes. We could see his heaviness. "You guys here on Prayer Mountain, I know you believe in prayer," he choked as he looked in our eyes. "Pray for my wife. She's been diagnosed with cancer. Doctor says it looks bad."

J.D. and I immediately stopped what we were doing and sat down on a park bench to pray with the man. Last I heard, his wife is still very much alive. But as he departed off down the hill, I was struck by a thought. I sure was glad I had not held enmity against that man. I remembered how J.D. had calmed me down with his long story about the code inspector and his manhole project. Sometimes we just need to cool it. It is good to have friends who help you recover focus—seasoned, mature friends.

Paul never hesitated to speak of his personal prayer life. My own prayer life grew significantly during these early construction years. Often frustrating burdens drove me to my knees. I did not at first understand what the Lord was doing with me, the time I spent in all the meetings with city and county officials poring over plans seemed like a waste. I admit to frustration in my spirit.

One night on my living room carpet I cried out, "Lord, I would like to spend more time in ministry." I visualized my nice desk and neat office, Bible open and a cup of coffee at hand. "O Lord, You've been good, but could you make it easier?" The Lord sometimes replies to me by giving me a scripture reference, a literal chapter and verse. Sometimes it's just the next verse down from what I am already pondering. He gave me John 13:7 that late night prayer session. "What I am doing you do not understand now, but you will know after this." This is the verse where Jesus corrected Peter who refused Jesus' bid to wash his feet.

It wasn't what I was asking for. But clearly the Lord wanted me to trust Him, even if I did not understand. Still I had a peace in that moment that what He was doing was unique. Later we would understand. Until then, we can cling to this promise: *All things are for our sakes…*(and for others)… *therefore we do not lose heart.*[16] It has been my privilege to carry everything to God in prayer.

God's way is often beyond our comprehension. Here is one such episode, which involves one of J.D.'s old friends—and dear to us, Van Dorsey.

A cold, steady, Seattle-like drizzle hung over the morning dampening the whole atmosphere. I was picking my way down into the soggy hollow on the south side of our hill. There were so many puddles of water here and there that I had to hopscotch randomly to find dry steps. This winter was turning out to be Dallas' wettest on record. Van Dorsey, close friend and retired heavy equipment operator, had come up on the mountain with his wife, Wanda. They were roughing it in a 19 foot camp and recreation trailer.

Van was digging us a thousand foot long trench for our sanitary sewer pipe. Because of the steep downhill route, he had engineered several down steps or "falls." He was working every day in the rain. The open ditch that led down toward the city sewer line had become more like an irrigation canal flowing full of rainwater.

Each step I took brought mud squishing up over my boots. I followed the revving sound of the tractor, making my way slowly down along the trench. The pungent smell of burnt diesel was heavy in the damp morning air. I dodged deep tire ruts filled with muddy water—a testimony of what our tractor was sloshing through.

Then I saw him. Sitting somewhat askew on the big caution-light colored rig, Van was precariously hanging on in the backward turned driver's seat. The whole rig was listing in an insecure, dangerous tilt. The Case tractor was stuck in mud all the way up to its belly and axles. Its outriggers were extended, but they too were partly submerged in the mire and mud.

Anxious concerns that the backhoe could topple over with Van hit me in the pit of my stomach. The unit's tilt seemed to worsen as I watched. I prayed desperately. Van was maneuvering the tractor with its boom and shovel. Inch by inch he was sliding it toward a giant, creek bottom elm tree. I had seen him push off from a tree at other times.

Van was a good equipment operator, an expert in fact. But today this water-logged creek bottom was merciless. In this bog he was handicapped beyond measure.

O God, I thought, this mud hole is whipping us. Isn't there anything You can do about the rain? Is the sun still up there somewhere? I was having my own private tiff with the Lord, the more I thought about it. God, You're such a stickler for every detail. You have rules for moons, Sabbaths, and equinoxes. You insist the Feast of Pentecost must be celebrated with leavened bread made from fresh flour on the day following the seventh Sabbath after Passover. But You seem so far removed and unconnected from the details of our struggle in real time. I tried hard to pray and "gird up the loins of my mind" in the admonition of the Apostle Peter. But the rain kept coming down. Drip, drip, drip, like Chinese water torture. Thirteen straight days of no sunshine. The persistent, pluvial clouds showed us no mercy. I struggled to think positive thoughts.

When Van glanced my way, I waved. I gave him a half-hearted thumbs up, feeling like a hypocrite when I did so. He shot back a big Van Dorsey grin at me, his hands glued to the controls. This guy, I couldn't help but think, is on the sheer edge of overturning—and he looks unconcerned, even confident. I struggled not to picture in my mind a worst case scenario. Doubt and fears mocked me.

Van was now sliding the tractor a yard at a time with its boom. He would gingerly pull in the outriggers in order to move the rig along. As it would tilt, he would steady it with the outriggers. It was a delicate tightrope balancing act. Finally, after agonizing moments, he was within boom's reach of the tree. As he pushed off the elm's big trunk, the stuck tractor got just enough traction to crawl out. It left behind a big wallow hole which looked like the muddy wallow of a herd of feral hogs in a Big Thicket swamp.

I wish I didn't agonize over things like this. But sometimes I do: If only God would give us a break and make the rain go away.

I was working my way over to Van when I realized a man had followed me down into the hollow and stood watching our show. He seemed bemused. It was quite a drama, the awkward tractor struggling down in the mud patch. I hailed the man with a wave. When he responded, I noticed he was dressed in the typical khaki and chambray shirt outfit which all the field guys from Dallas Water Utilities sport. Above the din of the diesel clatter, he was trying to tell me something. I cupped my ear toward him.

"Tell him," he hollered, "tell your guy he can park his rig. Y'all have dug enough. You can stop. We'll finish it. You're close enough. Finish getting your pipe in. We plan to come Monday and start the tap."

It was all so loud and backed up by engine noise that it took a few seconds for it to register in my mind. This city supervisor, who now is handing me his business card, is telling me the city will help us in this mess? In his Dallas drawl he went on to say, "No way y'all will ever get through that creek bottom with that rubber tire rig. We'll bring out a track hoe."

Sure enough, first thing Monday morning a sizable Dallas Water Utilities crew appeared on the mountain. They started by bringing in several big eighteen wheeler rock trucks dumping tons of crushed rock road base material. Large front loaders pushed the rock into an access lane for the city's heavy equipment. A mammoth track hoe arrived. It needed only twenty minutes or so to finish our digging job. Then it dug down to the city's buried pipeline. A work crew created a manhole. Three days later they smoothed down their site, gathered up the rock road and reloaded it into city trucks. Then they pulled out.

The supervisor stopped by to pay me a short visit. He admitted the rain and the mud made his job far more than routine. "I want you to tell your friends out here," he chuckled, "that y'all got the very last $850 sewer tap we'll ever do in these hills. Tell them the price has just gone up."

I know he meant it too. I know Dallas Water Utilities lost money on our deal. We paid only $850 to tie up a whole crew for the better part of the week.

This event was the culmination of two long years. And no one will ever even think about it when a commode is flushed on the mountain. To begin with we had originally been permitted for the installation of a sanitary septic system. But the large system, to meet city specifications, would have been expensive and would alter a good deal of the mountain top. It was not practical for us. So I set about to buy three acres below our hill where a city sewer line was available. We began drawing up a contract with the development company when that company suddenly went bankrupt in the Texas real estate bust of 1990.

Now the three acres we needed was transferred into the executorship and receivership of the Federal Deposit Insurance Corporation who, in turn, put it into the liquidation oversight of the Resolution Trust Corporation. The land seemed to slip far away from us.

For two years I had communicated with scores of government bureaucrats, slowly working my way through a virtual maze of the twenty-one lender banks involved. They were scattered over seven states. Many of these banks had failed and were reorganizing as new entities. Each one had to sign off on the deal. And here was the deal: When FDIC officials required us to obtain an official appraisal on the three acres, the appraisal came in valuing the property as having no real commercial worth. The land was too heavily encumbered with easements to be worth anything. Three easements existed: the Dallas Escarpment Zone (part of the greenbelt forest), a Dallas Water Utilities sewer easement, and the Texas Utilities aerial easement. FDIC then recommended it be sold to the church for "ten dollars and other considerations."

In the winter of 1992, we closed on the property in the hollow. The Oldham Little Church Foundation of Houston gave us a $2500 grant toward the sewer line cost. So as soon as we platted our present site with the new addition, we began. So did the rain. And when it rains, it pours.

One other big obstacle now confronted us. Dallas County sent us a tax bill for (gasp) $66,000! The developer's unpaid taxes, now in arrears, transferred to us when we became the new land owners. Only after four meetings with the Dallas Central Appraisal District and with the county tax assessor, were we able to settle our liability for a reasonable $366, a fraction of the developer's bill.

By now there was a much larger picture emerging of what God was doing. And it was of major importance. All those trips to Dallas City Hall: few people will ever know (or care) about all those meetings with city officials. Church building and developing ministry facilities were not new experiences for JoAn and me. When we had built out in the Texas Hill Country, the local officials in Comal County required only one permit for our job site. But in a big city like Dallas, there are typically twenty-seven different departments which pore over your plans and inspect every aspect of your work. Any one of those departments can shut down a construction project. And they often do. The reason is simple: more rules are required wherever more people live and congregate. This is especially true of public facilities. Every department, like the Dallas Fire Department for instance, wants to be assured your facility is safe and is built to code. My brother Don is a certified inspector and expert in city building codes. He answered hundreds of my questions about city codes and engineering.

Little by little, I began to make the acquaintance of those people who regulate and govern our city. The Lord began to teach me a clear lesson: If we were going to be "a prayer center for Dallas" we need to know first-hand the people and faces who make Dallas work as a city. The Lord fixed it in such a way I had to become personally acquainted with many of those people. I am glad He did.

In a thriving city, you will always find some encouraging public servants seated in authoritative offices. We found a few of them. One very helpful city staff leader was Elias Sassoones, Dallas' Assistant Director of Public Works. I believe that Elias was like Daniel in ancient Persia: he was divinely appointed. Speaking of Persia, Elias himself a Persian-born Jew was trained in Israel and in America. May the G-d of Israel richly bless him for the times he stood up for us when other department heads were ready to refuse us.

We have on many occasions prayed with our city fathers. I use the word "we" because I never go alone to pray where leadership is concerned. When I pastored out in the county, I knew almost no civic leaders. But now we routinely pray with mayors, city councilmen, district judges, county commissioners, county judges, district attorneys, chiefs of police, fire chiefs, sheriffs, as well as public school and university leaders.

The Lord convicted me that too many prayers people pray are generic prayers over generic needs. They are somewhat like the standard prayer, *Oh God, bless all the missionaries everywhere and please help the orphans.* Not much focus and passion involved. God did not raise up this prayer center for people to pray bland, impassive prayers for generic needs of a generic city.

Here is the key question every prayer ministry should ask: Who runs our city? Drives our buses? Keeps our airports working? Who puts out our fires? Who are the first responders to our emergencies? Who governs, makes laws, or even enforces them? Who feeds the poor? Runs our hospitals? What are their needs? Do we know? Do we even care? We should. And we should be burdened for them. We are obliged to pray for them. Especially those who hazard their lives for our safety.

What has emerged in the last fifteen to twenty years in the Dallas/Fort Worth area is a wealth of prayer alliances and spiritual fellowships among church leaders. These interceding, praying groups are constantly praying for the spiritual welfare of the city. They are in close touch with the real people and real-time needs of the city. What is new, the last decade or two, the Spirit has brought together the once separated regional, ethnic, denominational, and economic church groups. This has brought a new dimension of unity. The church is gathered for power. I have seen leaders from wealthy North Dallas megachurches prayerfully weeping alongside the Hispanic pastors from storefront ministries in the barrios of South Dallas. Without the prayers of fellow pastors, our own cause would have been lost. We thank them. We owe them a debt of love.

Often it has been our joy to host many such praying groups. This is our destiny. We were raised up for such a time as this. The Lord wants His church to be burdened for the city. He doesn't need abstract, generic, religious invocations. He wants real, heartfelt, passionate prayers. He wants the church to be what it was raised up to be: A house of prayer filled with people who care enough to weep over the hurts of the city and get involved in fixing it. As Jesus said, "A city on a hill cannot be hidden." We're called to be "the light of the world".[17]

Above all else a city needs a soul if it is to become a true home for human beings.
You, the people, must give it this soul.
–Pope John Paul

How Beautiful on the Mountains

Seek the peace and prosperity of the city—Pray to the Lord for it, because if it prospers, you too will prosper.
Jeremiah 29:7

CHAPTER NINE

BEAUTIFUL FOR SITUATION—THE PLAN

Beautiful for situation, the joy of the whole earth, is Mount Zion, on the sides of the north, the city of the great King.
Psalm 48:2

Every house is built by someone; but He who built all things is God.
Hebrews 3:4

It was on my 47th birthday, October 16, 1989, that we celebrated with dinner on the grounds. For us, a small but growing congregation, we had by God's grace reached an amazing milestone. We paid off the debt this week and burned the note on Prayer Mountain.

With great effort and many scratched up arms, we had cleared the brush thickets and prepared a building site. The new clearing opened up a compelling vista. To the west, Dallas' newest water reservoir and recreation area, Joe Pool Lake, impounded the waters of Mountain Creek. None of this, the 8000 acre lake and Cedar Hill State Park, was part of the scenario when we began this project. Now both were just a little more than a mile from our cliffs. Our promontory, standing 250 feet above the lake's blue water, was in the language of the Psalms "beautiful for situation." And in the valley directly below us, a new neighborhood of custom homes, Windridge, was being completed.

What could we build on this scenic site? We needed a good plan. In the winter of 1990, Arlon Conner, the architect who had drawn up the plans for the Church in the Wildwood (among others) drove up from Austin to familiarize himself with our building location. He brought with him his old gray-haired preacher dad who had for years manufactured church furniture. Together they measured our site, pulling their long tape in many different directions. We watched with fascination as they crisscrossed the grounds.

Arlon seemed to have a feel for the place. He proposed we build something that had a modest, natural Hill Country look to it. He didn't want to overpower the already beautiful hilltop. He had a concept which he sketched on paper. The worship center would add, not detract, from the high profile of the hill. He suggested it should appear to be a part of the hill—"as if it had grown up here quite naturally, like it had always been here." He encouraged us to work with wood and rock—and bring in the outdoors with plenty of big window views. The interior would have a living room feel to it. Arlon went back to the drawing boards in his studio. With his business partner Bobby Judd, they drafted the basic plan. Engineers were consulted to draft the foundation design. We had a set of construction prints by June of 1990.

As a congregation we were maturing with a sense of mission. We were becoming a team. The more we prayed together, the less we worried about our own needs and focused on those who were much less fortunate than we were. Charles, one of our prosperous businessmen, came back from Mexico with a passion to help the church there. He wanted to go to a slum community named Hidalgo, across the border from Laredo, Texas and assist a poor church there in laying a concrete floor. The current floor was dirt. JoAn also was stirred to rally our youth to go help. A few skilled builders in our congregation also got involved.

A minor division arose in the church. We had some good folk who felt we could ill afford this mission trip. Why were we going to another nation to work when we owned no facility for our own local work? Will we let our own project fall into neglect? Others in our congregation felt strongly in the principle of laying the foundation of being a true Great Commission ministry. We were called to be a going, gospel-spreading entity. Besides, we needed to believe that when we give, it shall be given back unto us. The latter opinion won out.

JoAn and the youth group put together a sizable work crew. She also handled the logistics, coordinating supplies both in Spanish and English. When the volunteers arrived in Hidalgo, the 107 degree summer heat was almost unbearable. They found thousands of miserably poor folk living in dirt floor cardboard and tar paper shanties. No electricity. No running water. These were totally dispossessed squatters, camped in *colonias* which stretched for miles along the Mexican National Railroad; "Calcutta poor" Mexicans subsisting almost within view of Texas' prosperity. Just across the river boundary.

Our team rolled up their sleeves and went to work. In the baking heat they got down and dirty and made things happen. The new church floor was completed in two days. On the third day they fanned out in small groups and ministered to needy families. They gave out groceries and children's toys. In their halting Spanish, our team spoke of the love of God and a personal Jesus, the Savior of all mankind. They returned home wilted and tired, but fulfilled. They sowed a foundation in Mexico.

Just two weeks later Cleddie Keith happened by Dallas and dropped in on our Wednesday evening prayer meeting out in the open air on the mountain. Cleddie said he sensed a "giving spirit" present. Accordingly, he offered the people an opportunity to give a special offering to install our foundation slab. We were just a small group that had gathered under the trees. But we witnessed a big miracle. We worshipped while whippoorwills sang. Then we raised an offering to pay for the slab. Thirty-three thousand dollars, in cash and pledges, came in that evening's offering. This was exactly what we needed to pay the foundation contractor who was now ready to install our slab. By July of 1990, we had our City of Dallas Building Permit. At last, the work on the batter boards for the foundation slab was beginning. And for us it was unusually impressive. We watched the workers' every move, like a bunch of sidewalk superintendents. The concrete and cable-tension workers could hardly believe we would bother to be spectators—watching them pour the foundation. But we were now so giddy with excitement. We even conducted a slab dedication service. As we finished this Sunday evening ceremony of praise and prayer, amazingly a bright rainbow appeared in the rain clouds over our heads. We were like children in our joy. This rainbow was surely a covenant sign unto us. A good sign in the heavens. On the foundation, JoAn had written scripture verses—while the concrete was setting up. On the south side under the platform she inscribed Psalm 24:3,4, *Who shall ascend into the hill of the Lord? Or who shall stand in His holy place? He that hath clean hands and a pure heart.*

On the west side where the big Palladian windows would be installed, she wrote Isaiah 56:7, *Even them will I bring to My holy mountain and make them joyful in My house of prayer…for Mine house shall be called a house of prayer for all people.*

Then on the north side which would be the front entrance, she put Psalm 90:17, *And let the beauty of the Lord our God be upon us; and establish Thou the work of our hands.*

We did not have long to celebrate. Only five days after the slab dedication service suddenly we were ordered to vacate our current leased meeting place and offices. The facility had been a great blessing to us. Located on Wheatland Road, Duncanville's busiest thoroughfare, it proved to be a place of high visibility. Our two years there had been a constructive period of growth. This attractive facility was owned by a local bank which bankrupted in the Texas real estate crash of '89-'90. When the Federal Deposit Insurance Corporation (FDIC) suddenly liquidated the property, we were given a 48 hour eviction notice. I pled with the FDIC officer for two extra days to move, which he grudgingly granted us. We moved out Labor Day, 1990. We set up a tent on part of the new slab. The goal now before us was to finish immediately the smaller Phase I plans which included offices, nursery, restrooms, and fellowship hall. We would leave the larger sanctuary for a later Phase 2 completion. The target date for occupancy was Christmas, 1990, an optimistic stretch. But it would not be an easy task. For the most part the weather cooperated with us. We experienced only a few rain-out days in autumn. The rain would seem to hold off all week until Saturday evening. But then it would come rolling in with vengeance. The storms seemed to take delight in leveling our meeting tent which we had erected on the slab. Invariably, the rain storm's pent up fury hit us on Saturday nights. One cannot imagine how helpless and hapless this made us feel on Sunday mornings. If there was any consolation, it was this: autumn on the mountain that year was exceptionally colorful. And everyone seemed to look forward to driving out to see the building's progress on a beautiful, fall colored hilltop. We would squeegee off water from the slab, raise the tent back up into its place and hold services. We were mostly a home cell church structured congregation. So our survival did not depend upon the Sunday morning gathering.

We did lose a few good families during those hardship days. It was never easy, and I can't blame anyone for leaving. No one was unkind about it. They offered other reasons for leaving. They were too nice to view us as peerlessly pitiful and inept. They just left us—and our tent. Looking back, I know that but for the grace of God we could not have survived as a viable ministry. Today we have infinitely more friends in various strong churches and denominations around us who would gladly make room in their facilities for us. We did ask two different congregations if we could rent their unused hall on Sunday evenings. Both turned us down. We were too new to have many close associations who could offer us help. We purposed back then that when we finally had our own facilities we would offer to assist other struggling ministries—as we would have so appreciated help. Any help at all. We have kept our pledge and aided many start-up ministries—most of which are still thriving. Healthy plants provide seeds for other new plants. Who knows, if we had rented an inexpensive place we might never have been willing to pay the price to move on with our building program.

As the framers raised up the walls of our Phase I fellowship hall, restrooms, nursery, and office, we began to plan for a Christmas on the Mountain event. By Thanksgiving Day our new building was completely closed in, but lacking the finished interior.

Following a gorgeous Indian summer autumn, winter came blowing in unseasonably cold in time for Christmas. Fortunately we had a beautiful big rock fireplace. But that is all the heat we had. We had installed central air and heat, but could not turn on the gas until our fire sprinkler system was signed-off by Fire Department code inspectors.

The day of the Christmas party, snow fell on the mountain. For a few days it looked like a winter wonderland. Snow covered everything. The rocky outcrops of the bluffs above the road were especially striking. Outlined in white and surrounded by tall snow-laden cedars, they presented a picture quite unlike Dallas, more like somewhere in the Rockies. Still, we were anxious that people would be reluctant to venture out in the cold. The opposite was true. Everyone wanted to catch a rare glimpse of snow on the heights. Children and adults alike came from nearby neighborhoods with all kinds of sledding devices—including rubber trash can lids—and sledded down the lane. Our gatherings had the appearance and atmosphere of an Aspen ski lodge party. We had a roaring fire in the fireplace, plenty of hot chocolate, and coffee. Much of Texas is generally warm and fair at Christmas time. Rarely do we experience anything like those snowy Christmas card Season's Greetings landscapes. This Christmas was different.

Desmond Evans, my personal pastor and highly regarded man of God, was our guest speaker. Standing near the blazing Yule Log, he had all of us pulling up a chair to hear him tell of the Wise Men who came from the East, following Bethlehem's star. He persuaded us wayfarers that we could succeed in our dream journey. Like the rallying pitch of a winning coach, he exhorted us to press on in our journey towards the goal. Our worn-down spirits were lifted by his message. But he also warned us. He reminded us that between their sighting of the bright star and the beholding of the Christ Child there were miles and miles of desert sand to traverse. "But Church," he said in his inimitable Welsh resonance, "the long journey shall be worth it all, worth the fantastic and splendid privilege of seeing Him!"

Our world doubled in 1990. So would our uncompleted facility. And we would finally begin to see action and answers to prayers which we had prayed (along with other Christians) for the advancement of God's Kingdom in the old oppressive Communist countries. In June of 1987, President Ronald Reagan had delivered a message, standing at the Brandenburg Gate by the Berlin Wall. He spoke to the whole world and to the Premier of the Supreme Soviet and leader of the Soviet Union (USSR) when he challenged him, "Mr. Gorbechev, if you want peace, open this gate! Tear down this wall!"

In the next two years, freedom uprisings spread through the Eastern Bloc nations like wildfire. First in Poland, then Czechoslovakia, Hungary, East Germany, Ukraine, Georgia, Romania, and ultimately in the Baltic states. One by one, nations ousted their despotic Communist bosses. The Evil Empire crumbled and along with it, the obstacles and prohibitions against the gospel. JoAn and I had been in Western Poland in August of 1989 when the news came of Communism's fall in Warsaw. Three days later we were in Prague, Czechoslovakia when that awful Communist government collapsed like Humpty Dumpty falling off the wall. The Wall in Berlin also came down.

So our energy in early 1990 was devoted to sending prompt aid missions to formerly underground churches in many of these nations. The pace of the work on our Prayer Mountain facility slowed as a result. But slowly and surely it began to take on the beauty of craftsmanship. Our own local talent played a key role in finishing the interior. The winter of '91 was a time of advancement and completion. In late January we held our first wedding reception in our new fellowship hall—my son's. Kipling had been traveling as band leader in a contemporary Christian music group known as the Margaret Becker Band. In Oklahoma he had met the love of his life, Valerie. A smart, beautiful blond like he had always wanted, Valerie had grown up in a large Baptist church in Oklahoma City. There they were married. After a short honeymoon, they came back through Dallas for their reception where Kip had earlier helped trail-blaze our beginnings.

A new optimism filled our now-growing congregation. There was even a fresh air of dignity about our gatherings. We had finally won some victories—by God's grace. Things began to work better. Nick, our missionary/rock mason from Montana labored through the cold days of winter finishing a masterful work of art in stone on the new facility. He refused to let cold weather delay him. "Cold weather is something," he would declare, "you people don't experience here." He didn't even wear a heavy jacket. "There's no excuse for not showing up to work on a day as comfortable and fair as today!" It was 25 degrees F. Nick was often the only man working on cold days. The rock that Charlie Rodgers quarried was now a beautiful building, thanks to Nick Trout. Charlie would be proud. Real proud.

Spring of '92 brought us a long season of beautiful weather. Wildflowers bloomed profusely in the meadow at the base of the mountain. Inside our new fellowship hall, we were applying finishing touches. We intentionally left the adjacent kitchen unfinished. In place of cabinet works were chairs. We needed the extra seating space for the growing congregation. Easter Sunday picnic on the grounds was like a homecoming and a picturesque festival. Some of my favorite photographs are from that day.

In May we were contacted by our city councilman and friend, Dr. Charles Tandy, an anesthetist for Methodist Hospital system. Steve Bartlett, Dallas' young conservative mayor, wanted to hold a Town Hall meeting up on the mountain for our new neighborhood. Dr. Tandy was very enthusiastic about this event.

I explained to him, and to the Mayor's office, that we were operating under a temporary Certificate of Occupancy, only allowing for Sunday gatherings. The permanent Certificate of Occupancy (C.O.) was pending completion of a paved road and parking area. Officials there told me not to worry about the C.O. problem. Our meeting was scheduled for the first week in June. On June 2, Dallas Building Inspection granted us our permanent Certificate of Occupancy. We framed it and displayed it the very day it arrived in the mail.

By September we were finally completing Phase 1. We now had a beautiful place to meet. We were getting ready to launch Phase 2 when a group of folk grew critical and discontented. We found ourselves caught in a desperate struggle for spiritual unity. Where had our brotherly agreement gone? In a congregation, agreement is a prerequisite for divine solutions.[18]

In the heat of summer, and in the vacation time absence of congregational prayer gatherings, serious dissension had set in. Attempts at unity broke down. As our prayer meetings flatlined, so also did the work falter. Where we had once been a people of the Word, we were becoming merely a wordy people. We were driven apart by various opinions.

Unity is such a precious commodity in the community of faith. Kingdom decisions are much too crucial in scope, too eternally weighty in their impact, to be decided outside the arena of unified prayer. After all, we had been birthed as a ministry of prayer—not as a ministry of talk! The long talks that summer led nowhere.

Debate centered around what we should do with the cash proceeds realized from the recent sale of a donated home. We had been given a rent house to sell expressly for funding our building program. It was, to be sure, a *fixer upper*. The property was not ready to go on the market. However, its surrounding neighborhood was stable and in a desirable middle income location. It had potential. Schools and shops were nearby.

JoAn and her dad, Jofred Holder, were eager to advance our stalled mountain chapel project. They readily volunteered to take on the needed renovation—without pay. Both of them, along with some hired help, put in three months of hard sweat equity on that house. Finally the dwelling was clean and remodeled. It was marketed as a "charming three bedroom, two bath home." It actually had curb appeal. Its sale fetched a good price, putting much needed cash into our depleted building fund.

To be sure, this was an energizing breakthrough for JoAn and me. We now had about half the amount of money needed to cover the cost of those wooden arch beams and decking, all of which made up the next big phase of our construction. Our goal now seemed close and obtainable. I gathered the church board. This was a leading moment, I assured them. Our people needed to see progress where we had too long been stalled. The price of lumber was rising daily due to a massive and unusual snowstorm in late winter which laid waste to millions of acres of timber in the southern yellow pine forests. Countless trees were flattened to the ground and inaccessible. Speculators were driving prices of rare lumber supplies higher each day.

"I believe we need to step out in faith," I urged the men, "and lock in the price on those beams by sending a down payment to the company." The men balked. I was caught off guard. Our small board feared that ordering the engineered wood structures would put us in jeopardy. We would end up in debt to the manufacturer, Wood Systems Inc. of Alabama. Sure the company had made us a very reasonable price offer, even agreeing to give us a three month interest free payout. This begged the question of what would we do in ninety days from now if the product is ready to be delivered and we have no money to get it out of layaway. They had a point, maybe.

I responded. Every act of faith requires of us in some way to step out in faith. This venture may look like a risk to us. For instance, Peter's stepping out of the boat toward Jesus. We were not talking about utilizing some gimmick to presume upon God's miraculous supply. A principle of faith is a prepared heart, a willingness to hear and move forward on the Word even if it moves us into the unknown. The one caveat is this: *When your moment of truth comes, the time of preparation is too late.* I could see plainly that we had not been praying together. We were not in unity. We were not prepared to move forward in faith. The men were firm in their decision to put off the order "till later."

JoAn was absolutely crushed, shaken to the core by their decision. "I feel like quitting," she told me. "If all my hard work has been for nothing, what's the use? I did all the work, but I was never once consulted, nor did my opinion count on how to use the money." She had a point, I consoled her. But it was useless to proceed without unity. And we did not have it.

Obviously the summer '92 was a thorny time for us. It was our *Summer of Discontent.* This ungraciousness from our board seemed to be a national malady as well. Our nation was preparing to turn out our sitting President following his executing the victorious Persian Gulf War and his rescuing the Kuwait oil supply. So it goes with human nature.

Still, God has a way of bringing forth roses from our thorns. The divisive decision to put off the order for the beams turned out to be a moot question. The men who doubted and countered my leadership grew increasingly discontented. They left us on the first Sunday of September, inviting others to follow them out. They wanted their own work. Their ambition would have to be tempered by reality. And it was. Splits never end well because they do not begin right.

I had almost missed the signals. In order to keep the bond of peace, we blessed those who pulled out with a love offering and supplies as we sent them along their way. It was with deep, mixed emotions that we watched a third of our congregation leave. Des Evans reassured me and challenged me to forgive and let it go. "Where pride exists," he exhorted, "everyone is a leader and no one follows."

Even more piercing to my soul was the sudden death of a close pastor friend, José Diaz, who died only days after the group left. He suffered a massive heart attack while out jogging. José had loved Prayer Mountain. He envisioned great things for the hill even when it was still in the rough. He was a man of prayer. So we often prayed together early in the morning. José coached me in Spanish. Under his tutelage my vocabulary grew until I was quite conversant. He always chuckled good heartedly whenever I used the wrong word. He helped me learn words that are difficult for *gringos* to pronounce. I urged him to utilize his gifted wife, Manuela, in his services more often. That was a big, welcomed step forward for a Hispanic male leader. At his funeral we sang one of José's favorite old hymns:

Estoy listo si el me llama,
Estoy listo si el me llama.
Estoy listo si el me llama.
Estare en la viña del Señor.
The English version is worded a bit differently:
When He calls for me I will answer.
When He calls for me I will hear.
When He calls for me I will answer
I'll be somewhere a-listening for my name.[19]

I left the cemetery that sweltering hot afternoon. The Spanish words rang in my heart: "Estoy listo si el me llama." (I am ready if He calls me.) I drove back to the hill, little knowing that the days ahead would suddenly turn bright and busy with blessing after blessing.

Des Evans came back to visit me on the hill. Des is a well-seasoned, widely respected pastor and conference speaker. When he speaks people listen. His assessments are received with a good deal of esteem. He is blunt-spoken. A strong Welsh clip adds sharpness to his speech. Being well acquainted with building program stresses and losses, he was in sympathy with me. A partly empty slab stood as a mute challenge to what appeared to some as a far-fetched dream.

We walked out in front of the large empty slab where the sanctuary was planned. There we halted to pray over it. Then Des began to quote scripture and speak encouragement over my sagging spirit. He greatly lifted my hopes.

"These hands have laid the foundation of the house," he proclaimed in full assurance, quoting from Zechariah 4:9. He lifted my hands along with the spoken divine promise, "These hands also shall finish it: and you will know that it is the Lord's doing."

I knew when he left that the Lord had sent him. I also was assured we could finish the work. Still I had no idea how quickly things would now move. As a congregation we were smaller. But the discord was gone and we were all finally in one accord. We doubled in size by the end of the year! Des returned just 21 months later to consecrate our bright new sanctuary. It was debt free and dedicated as "a house of prayer for all nations." To God be the glory!

If the Boards of the churches would only learn to spend more time with God and less time debating, they could save all those midnight meetings where everybody leans back weary from discussing things. I tell you, you can cut down your time in debating and discussing if you spend more time waiting on God.
–A. W. Tozer[20]

If the Mountain Could Speak

A bad cause requires many words.
–A German Proverb

The ways of God are full of surprise. He chooses the unexpected, and is always doing the impossible. The theologians of Israel had a great deal of trouble with their God, for they never could keep Him orthodox.
Samuel Chadwick, from *Through the Year With Samuel Chadwick*[21]

CHAPTER TEN

LET US RISE UP AND BUILD

Take for yourselves twelve stones from here...You shall carry them over with you and take for yourselves twelve men from the people...and command them saying, leave them in the lodging place...
Joshua 4:2,3

Let us rise up and build.
Nehemiah 2:18

Almost immediately a deep settled peace and optimism swept over the faithful of our congregation. I no longer had the hollow feeling of futility, like I was a bus driver motoring his coach up to the mountaintop of glory, but at every bus stop some folk would get off. Other folk would get on. It was pointless to try to convince some riders to stay aboard. It dawned on me that this was not even my job. I'm just the motorman, the bus driver. Come with me, if you like. But I will not back up nor delay in order to try and win you over. This bus is going all the way to the summit.

The next Sunday we got down on our knees literally as a congregation. We thanked God for the fact that we were all in one accord about proceeding. A new confidence took hold and filled our meetings with enthusiasm. No longer would decisions be made by opinions and limited mindsets. We wanted God's heart. We were back to prayer, willing to wait upon Him for guidance.

The very same Sunday (following the group's departure) four new families came in, speaking of their willingness to serve the vision of the house. These were people of good training and mature spiritual giftings. Typical of this refreshing company was the Gran Porter family. Gran was an experienced architect who specialized in designing public facilities. We pored over our building plans together. He loved them as well as our unique site. He pointed out the need to update the three year old drawings. He started promptly reworking the plans. Gran reinforced our enthusiasm for the deal we had on those big manufactured beams. "Glue lams" he called them. We wasted no time in ordering those beams.

We were none too soon. Everything had changed overnight in the building trades industry. The price of lumber was skyrocketing. The vice president of our Alabama supplier told me if I had waited one more week he would have had to void our agreement and issue us a much higher price quote. All this was due to the disastrous effect of Hurricane Andrew.

In late August of 1992, Hurricane Andrew moved across the Bahamas as a Category 2 storm. Yet by the time it hit the coast of Southern Florida at Homestead, it was a monster Category 5 hurricane. It barely missed Miami. Andrew's 150 mile per hour winds literally leveled Homestead. Tens of thousands were left homeless, the city devastated. Then the storm swept across southern Florida and moved out into the warm waters of the Gulf of Mexico. It then took dead aim at Louisiana. Morgan City was blasted with 135 mph hurricane force winds. There again was total devastation and loss of life.

The news media termed this storm "The 27 Billion Dollar" hurricane. It was the costliest storm (prior to Katrina) to ever hit the United States. The building suppliers quickly ran out of everything needed for rebuilding. Overnight, lumber prices doubled. For instance, at our job site 4'x8' oriented strand board (OSB), the basic framing material for construction, went from $9.00 per sheet to $19.00 per sheet, if it could be found at all. Because we had already paid for their engineered drawings, the owners of Wood Systems Inc. kept their promise on our price. Thankfully. It was a miracle. They later told me they made no profit on those big glue laminated beams, which now stand as pillars in our mountain chapel.

In the autumn of '92, more new families poured in to our church. We were meeting now in what was designed to be our fellowship hall. For our annual October 19th celebration (of becoming deed holders of the mountain) I had scheduled Jim Mackey to speak. Our hall was packed to the walls. Jim spoke to us that we were now in a time of "fresh grain, oil, and new wine" from Joel 2:21-28. His message greatly encouraged us. What's more, Jim's marvelous, friendly manner fit us like a glove. We enjoyed dinner on the picnic grounds. The very next week, the congregation Shepherd Springs, led by Jim and his wife Lynette, merged with our work. It was a match made in heaven.

Jim had pastored a major denominational fellowship in our city. Jim and I, as friends, had prayed together about his calling to the nations and to speaking, an apostolic role than a pastoral one. When he resigned his local pastoral office, he was approached by quite a few parishioners who vowed their commitment to follow him into his new work. That small group grew to include others, mostly new believers. Jim continued to move into his new anointing. He loved his work in distant places like China, Ukraine, Romania, and Nigeria. But with all his busy planting and watering in God's garden, Jim still felt responsible to find a permanent home for his followers. He found that place at Mountain Creek Church. The new people immediately became one with us. This included Jim and Lynette and family. Jim's apostolic gifting has benefitted us more than words can express. *God who comforts the downcast, comforted us by the coming of* Jim Mackey and family. [22]

With the New Year in 1993, it was time for a new beginning. A call went out to all the men of our congregation to come seek the Lord in prayer until late that night. Our five presbytery leaders were requested to come in from their various places. We needed them to minister and pray with us. Each of them, being seasoned ministers, was asked to seek the grace of God for guiding wisdom concerning our future.

That evening our missions presbyter, Syvelle Phillips, came straight from the DFW airport on a return flight from India. Rene Brown came from his home in North Dallas. (He would be departing for work in Kenya in a few weeks.) Des Evans had just returned from Panama. Jim Mackey came in from Colorado. Our two other presbyters sent messages by telephone. To a man they all had the very same word. In fact, they were led to declare some of the same Bible verses. It was now time for us to cross over and possess our *promised land*. A door of hope and opportunity was now opened before us. We finally enjoyed an unprecedented spirit of unity and agreement—well beyond what we had ever experienced before. The harmony of brothers in unity was both good and pleasant. It was like the Book of Acts which uses the term "one accord" thirteen times. Unity is followed by answered prayer.

At the conclusion of the powerful, stirring prayer time together, we felt the Spirit's leading to monument the evening. We set up stones we gathered from the mountain on the slab, building an altar. Twelve large stones in all. That stone altar was a physical manifestation of our recommitment and agreement to press on with our original vision. We would build, we would be a House of Prayer. We would build by faith, through prayer.

When a divine vision is given, its fulfillment rarely comes like one envisioned it to be. We may imagine and dream of how it will unfold. But we cannot count on it happening just as we hoped it would. Be careful of presumptions. In Acts 16, the Apostle Paul had a dream of a man in Macedonia crying out, "Come over and help us." Arriving in Macedonia, Paul and Silas found no man. They hoped to establish a church there. They began by sharing the gospel and praying with women down by a brook. Their deliverance ministry in Philippi landed them in jail—and beaten up at that. As they sang hymns to God at midnight, the Lord intervened. An earthquake brought the missionaries both a loosening of chains and a face to face showdown with their jailer. The conflicted warden surrendered to the Lord, and his whole family was baptized. From a small, painful beginning, the church there at Philippi went on to become Paul's crown jewel of missionary endeavors. The Lord has a wonderful way of bringing good things out of our pain and disappointments, like roses growing among thorns.

In early 1993 the work on the mountain progressed at a rapid pace. We managed to pay off the balance due on the beams—all except the C.O.D. delivery fees on their truck shipment to us. The company called to inform us they could no longer warehouse our beams. It was time to erect them. The C.O.D. bill was $6800. The beams were coming our way. Now.

JoAn and I had tossed and turned all night in a fitful sleep. We had no idea where we would get $6800 first thing the next morning. The afternoon before, we had been telephoned by Wood Systems Inc. of Greenville, Alabama and told the shipment of our manufactured "glue lam" beams and all the tongue and groove decking had been loaded and the trucks had left their yards. They were headed for us in Dallas. The erector crew and crane would meet them in the morning. We would need to pay the drivers $6800 for the remaining freight/hauling fee before any of the material could be off-loaded. Our bank account was near zero. We had spent all we could scrape together to pay off the remaining balance due on the beams and decking lumber. Our credit card was maxed out. We hardly had six dollars and eighty cents between us—much less $6800!

When we drove out to the mountain early in the morning, we could see the raised boom of the giant erector crane. From the street below, the boom looked like a signal tower on the hilltop. We knew the work crew was there and ready to go. We arrived in our offices, looking as normal as ever, as if we could walk right in to the finance office and casually write out that $6800 check. We had wealthy connections in high places. But our pockets were empty.

The truck drivers had left the hill to grab a quick bite of breakfast. We knew we had 30 minutes or so to come up with the money. The staff came in at 9:00 am. We pulled them into a huddle for prayer. I read from Jesus' words in Matthew 18:19, "Again I say to you that if two of you agree on earth concerning anything that they ask, it will be done for them by My Father in heaven."

God alone was the answer. We had run out of human resources. Meager resources at that. We quickly got down to the business of prayer. While we were in our office praying, we looked up to see one of the single ladies in our fellowship coming up the walkway. Through the window I could recognize Diane. Good! She could help us pray, I thought. She was a woman of prayer and serious intercession. I invited her into my office to join our staff prayer huddle.

Diane responded, "First let me be obedient to the Lord." She handed us a check. "The Lord told me to bring this check in now and not wait until the Sunday offering." She handed us a check made out to Mountain Creek Church. The amount was $6800! We were speechless. Absolutely stunned! "This is a tithe on my insurance settlement," Diane reminded us, "on the collision I suffered when that truck ran a red light. The settlement check came in yesterday's mail." That incident had occurred well over two years previous to this day. It was a dim memory to me, which I had actually forgotten.

Our staff prayer meeting erupted into joyful praise and thanksgiving to *Jehovah Jireh*, our Provider. No way we could have coordinated a better synchronized ending to a real pressure situation. There was even some repenting of anxious doubts. We've learned through these tests to rest on His promises. His eye is on the sparrow and He watches over us. He is an on-time God.

The big wood beams were erected that day. The Lord faithfully was moving toward the day we would consecrate the house of prayer on the mountain.

Grace works. Grace abounds and abounding prevails. It is something more than a smile of good nature, a sentiment of pity, an amiable complacency. Grace is thought, emotion, power. It redeems, conquers, saves. Grace goes over the trail of sin, destroys its power, undoes its mischief, and turns its weapons to its own destruction.
–Samuel Chadwick[23]

CHAPTER ELEVEN

THE ROAD

A highway shall be there, and a road…the redeemed shall walk there.
Isaiah 35:8,9

Miracles are the swaddling clothes of infant churches.
–Thomas Fuller

How the steep drive up our hill went from a rough mule train road to Prayer Mountain Lane is a miracle story. An absolute miracle. A bit of misery and mystery, but in the end a great miracle.

JoAn and I would often walk up that rising ten percent grade, the whole 1400 feet of it, huffing and puffing and praying for a better road. We started with a real challenge: a bulldozed old jeep trail to the top. This lane dated back to the days when this hill was the high point of a 3500 acre mule ranch. Its owner was an eccentric millionaire who loved and raised prized mules. He would train his twenty-mule teams to pull cargo wagons, just for show in parades and rodeos. The road up the mountain, although rougher than a washboard and awfully eroded, was just good enough for his mule trains. Only a four wheel drive vehicle could manage to travel up it.

About the time we purchased this hill, a curiosity-seeking off-road driver came exploring out here in his brand, spanking new blue and silver (Dallas Cowboys colors) Chevy Silverado pickup truck. I was at the bottom of the hill trying to patch a deep rut which had a seep draining down through it. He drove up and lowered his power window to ask if he could venture up to the top. I stepped closer and responded to this slim-faced guy who sported a Cowboys' ball cap, worn backwards. I didn't mind his driving up, I told him. Most folk don't bother to ask. But I tried to warn him away. Especially should he not risk his new Chevy on this rough course. Dismissing my counsel with a smile, he assured me his new truck could go just about anywhere. It was an idle boast. He took off. Ten minutes later he came walking back sheepishly whipped. He had practically demolished his new Silverado. He got caught in a deep rut while coming down. It led him just like a train track on down against a limestone embankment. I saw tears of remorse in his eyes. I felt sorry for him. He was warned.

Incidents like this made JoAn and me wonder. We want people to come to the mountain. But how will they come if they can't even get up the hill? Jim Williams, my upscale developer friend walked up with me one morning. "Robert," he said frankly, "I see $100,000 you'll need here before you ever get started." So big a need. So small a congregation! God help us, we prayed.

Help was forthcoming. Enter Mike Wallace, the civil engineer in charge of the field work for the big development company. When they began building a network of city parkways and neighborhood streets out here, they first tore out an old asphalt road. Mike, being a devout Believer, was in sympathy with our prayer center ministry. He had the Mario Sinacola Inc. road building crew haul the old asphalt and spread it on our lane. "Gotta put it somewhere," he apologized. He engineered and personally stayed after hours to excavate a new turn in our road. This made for a more natural approach to this new city parkway, Eagle Ford Drive; a less severe rise as well. He had that recycled asphalt sheep tracked (mechanically) into our well packed road base. Our new road was a "freebie." Still a bit rough, it was quite passable for our pioneer beginnings. At least no more Chevy pickups in the ditch!

Later, in July of '92, Tom Burlingame came to be our night watchman and handyman. He was a skilled young man who had overseen some Youth With A Mission projects. He kept telling me he could easily upgrade our road. He had a plan. I'm thinking *big bucks* in cost. Sure. But in the fall of '92, a fresh very positive faith-filled attitude gripped us all. I repented and talked it over with Tom. He had a background in road construction, he recounted to us. Recalling his youthful years being reared in Western New York's Catskill Mountains, he told how his father, a county road and bridge supervisor taught him everything about road building. Tom already had all his prices lined up. He would even call Waco or Houston to see if he could get a better deal on equipment rental.

"Tom, it's too far to go to Houston," I told him. "Get it here." He nodded and went over his plan. He claimed he could remake our road for less than $4000.

It looked manageable. It wasn't expensive. However, everything beyond our operating budget, which included our missions commitments, went into finishing the chapel building. We could stretch somehow. So I urged Tom to get started. He rented heavy equipment. He had about twenty long bed, tandem truckloads of crushed recycled concrete hauled in. He added to this mix at least a hundred 90 pound sacks of Portland cement. He spread the material with a maintainer grader. A friend began to hose it down with water. Then a light rain set in, which Tom said was perfect weather. He packed the material down firmly, running up and down the lane on a heavy vibrating roller. Tom loved it. The activity brought back his youthful memories of growing up in the mountainous region of New York. We all were pleasantly surprised at the results. For a bit less than $4000 we now had a wide, smooth road. It even looked like a real road.

Shortly afterward, Tom was called back to his Catskill Mountain hometown to care for his ailing father. We planned a send-off reception for him after Sunday evening's service. One of our praying saints felt led to buy Tom a new suit. I had mixed emotions about this gift. After all, I had bought him two or three new sport shirts. He loved his old worn threadbare tee shirts. He felt more comfortable in the kind of tee shirts that I would retire to the garage as polish rags. Not wanting our watchman to look destitute, I tried to finesse him into the new threads. He obviously didn't care for my *glad rags*. But I was wrong about him.

Amazingly, Tom showed up Sunday in his new suit, shirt, and tie. He was sporting a real haircut and a fresh shave. His old shoes were shined to military specs. Honestly, most of us did not recognize him at first glance. One member even asked, "Tom, is that you?" We were stunned. This friend was going back to New York transformed. He was one new man! He left early the next morning with his faithful dog Dipstick at his side in his old step van truck turned SUV. He even was wearing one of those sport shirts I gave him.

Tom's renovated road served us well for the next eighteen months of heavy construction. Still, we all knew the inevitable fact: Before we could get city occupancy permission for the chapel, we would need a city approved road. Jim Williams, my friend, had proved correct. A hundred thousand dollars is what we needed. I had two different bids in my desk drawer. Where would we get $100,000 beyond what our chapel costs? The amount seemed huge in 1993. Lord, where would we get that kind of money?

We kept walking the lane and praying. And trying to figure out a plan. God would have to do the impossible.

September of '93, just a year after Tom had improved Prayer Mountain Lane, a white Chevy Suburban came driving up our road. From our front offices, JoAn could see four men in business suits get out. They walked up our front walk to be greeted by my mom. Also, JoAn came out to welcome them. (I was in Fort Worth, by God's design, attending a ministry conference.)

These men introduced themselves as department heads from Texas Utilities power company. They have transmission lines on the east boundary of our hilltop. They asked to tour our unfinished shell of the chapel. They wondered aloud as to when we would expect a finished date.

JoAn's answer was real and practical. "When the Lord supplies," she replied. "When He sends us the money, we will finish it."

They smiled an expression of being both intrigued and bemused. They were not accustomed to operating on that kind of business plan.

"We need to talk to you about your road," they said, getting down to business. "We need a new power substation built up here next door to you. The only way to access it is to utilize your road. But we'll need to upgrade it."

JoAn countered, "It will need to be paved."

"Well, we usually just lay down a gravel surface," one of the engineers explained. Others nodded in agreement. They were all very courteous and businesslike.

JoAn clarified her statement about the paved road. "It is a city code requirement for us to have paved access to the church. It is a public building." She continued to shed light on our need. "Besides, we've tried gravel roads. After the first big rain, all the gravel washes down the hill. The road needs to be paved."

"Well, we've never done paved roads. But maybe it can be done…" the key man seemed to be thinking out loud. "So do you see us both sharing the cost?"

"Certainly," JoAn agreed.

Their lead spokesman continued to press the issue. "And how would we share? Something like half and half?"

"No," JoAn replied in a friendly tone. "You are big and we are small.

You 75, us 25 percent," she replied with a smile, gesturing with her hand pointing to the group, then back to herself.

At this the men chuckled politely, glancing at each other. To JoAn's sharing concept, they responded, "It's something we've never done. But we'll have to talk this over. Then next week we'll get in contact with you." They then departed in a mannerly fashion.

It was best that I was not there. I was so very desperate for a road I certainly could not have been coy about it. I would have jumped at the *half and half* offer, although I would then have had no clue in the world how to meet my obligation. Thank God for an administrative wife. We visionaries need someone who will fill in the blanks.

Two weeks later the contract came to us via courier. Terms of the contract: Texas Utilities pays 75%; we pay 25% for a paved road! Engineered drawings and surveys to begin right around my birthday in mid-October. Road work will commence April 1, 1994. Our part financially will be due upon completion of the work. For me this was a huge birthday present from the Lord. Huge! We were going to have a miracle road.

The rest of the story gets better, even though it is filled with suspense. In May we sent out hundreds of engraved invitations for the Consecration of House to be on July 3rd. We had counted on the road's completion in May.

But it wasn't until May that the road work even began. May was rainy. There were delays. The work continued off and on into June. The crew would leave. Then come back in two weeks to do more work. And then it went into July! We had begun to wonder: will we even have a completed road for people to drive up for Consecration Sunday?

Finally a brand new Prayer Mountain Lane was finished and the traffic barriers removed on July 2. This was only one day prior to the Consecration of the House. This long delayed project had us really sweating.

It was a professional job, entirely overseen by the engineers of Texas Utilities. Now it was finished. Our contract with the utility company stipulated that our 25% share became due "upon completion." But we did not have a money figure. No bill. No bottom line amount. I kept waiting for some accounting. A reckoning.

A month later and no bill had come. Then two months and still no statement, no invoice arrived. I began to dread the moment an envelope would arrive in the mail which would present us with a whopping $25,000 bill due upon receipt. We had expended ourselves finishing the chapel. We enjoyed the great new road every day. But I thought about that bill every time I drove up the hill. Months passed. I couldn't put it off any longer. I picked up the phone to call that key Texas Utilities executive. I had his cell phone number, his card. He was out in West Texas when he answered my call. I could hear his automobile's background noise.

"Pastor, what do you need?" he asked me, responding a bit abruptly.

"I never got a bill from your company," I answered.

"I'm not in billing!" he shot back.

"No. I mean a bill on the new road we share. I don't know what we owe you," I continued.

"Oh, that road!" he recalled. "Pastor, you won't get a bill. We talked it over. We need that road. You don't owe us for it. Just don't call me about it again. It's okay. We intended to bless the church."

"You've got my word," I exclaimed. "You'll not hear from me again on this issue!" You bet I never called him back, as per his request. And he was correct. We never got that bill. Ever.

A hundred thousand dollar road. A gift from the power company—and the Lord Who Supplies. A miracle road.

We were, in a small way, able to return the blessing to Texas Utilities. When we later purchased the wooded hill to the east of their power substation, we provided them an alternate access to their substation. Saddle Ridge Road, which runs through our land, is fairly level. This is important. Every few years Dallas gets a winter ice storm. Our winter weather is more a matter of ice than of snow. Ice is not good for accessing the mountain because Prayer Mountain Lane goes right up the north face of the mountain. It is definitely treacherous and impassable in ice. Now, in emergencies, the power company can access their plant through our alternate Saddle Ridge Road entrance.

Over the years we have become good neighbors—and a good team. After all, we are both in the power and light business. And we travel the same road.

It is a fact of our history that our very first two organizational Sunday meetings were held in the local power and light company auditorium.

Someone in our group suggested we name our new congregation *The Power and Light Church*. More rational minds prevailed. We named it Mountain Creek Community Church with an aim to locating in the new community of Mountain Creek. But we are definitely in the power and light ministry. That is what the gospel is all about! Jesus "the light of the world."[24] Christ "the power of God...and the wisdom of God."[25]

A year or two after the new road was opened, I noticed a construction crew working over at the power substation. I strolled over there and struck up a conversation with the man in charge, the line patrolman. He lived in my neighborhood, I discovered. In our friendly talk, he threw in a "by the way," querying me about the road.

"You got friends in high places," he asserted. Then he added a punch line. "You got this beautiful paved road running all the way through your property. It stops dead at our property line. The rest of the way it's crushed rock right up to our plant gate. How'd you do that? Headquarters is not known for putting in pavement. You must know someone really high up."

I nodded in agreement, not wanting to tell him the story. I had been asked to keep it quiet. "We have a friend in high places," I responded, pointing my finger heavenward. "The Most High place."

He smiled. I believe he got the connection. He never brought it up again.

"I will even make a road in the wilderness..."
Isaiah 43:19

I took the road less traveled by
And that has made all the difference.
–Robert Frost, *Stopping by Woods on a Snowy Evening*

CHAPTER TWELVE

CONSECRATION OF THE HOUSE

For every house is built by some man but he who built all things is God.
Hebrews 3:4

In 1993 the acceleration of miracles continued. The local congregation was in a period of thriving growth. In the old Communist East Europe nations (the former Soviet Union) a great and effectual door of opportunity existed for the gospel, but there were many adversaries. We had suffered a setback in late '92 when one of our leading missionaries put us through the awful pain of betrayal, leaving his wife and mission for a new found Ukrainian love. But like an Alpine meadow, when the spiritual rains of '93 came in the East, all the seeds of the past sowing began to flower magnificently. Steve and Kristi Weber, part of our own family, emerged as respected leaders of the Christian Broadcasting Network in Kiev, Ukraine. Our tears of sacrifice had not been in vain.

Finally the chapel on the mountain was beginning to look finished. We had a tall spire and cross custom made for the chapel. It would be the finishing touch, architecturally, standing atop the high lantern structure of the rooftop. It was 18 feet in height. This caused our job supervisor to fret over how he would ever get it up and fastened in its place. It was quite heavy. So it sat in its crate outside near the back door of our edifice.

This bothered one of our key men, John Wright. He was a retired engineer. He kept after me to get that spire up. John was like a dog with a bone in that he would not let it go. In the spring of '94, John and I prayed together about the matter. He was a dear friend and supporter, but I felt badgered. I had no idea how we would get that unit up there, except for hiring a thousand-dollar-per-hour rig and operator.

"But God," John would confess, "He's able!"

Shortly after we prayed in agreement together, John happened to be grocery shopping at a local supermarket. He paused to observe a work crew hoisting up a big new sign atop the store. Our friend John has an unconventional, inquisitive nature. He wants to know how everything works. While marveling at the big hoist boom truck, he noticed the sign company's name on the truck included a fish logo. He took this as a sign from God. John never meets a stranger. He approached the crew leader as a brother and discussed our plight with him, describing our cross and spire. He probably gave him his best estimate of its size and weight. He was big on details.

As God's grace would have it, the sign supervisor was a committed Christian. He agreed to help John during his lunch break. If John would arrange for hamburgers for his three helpers, they would come over to our hilltop for lunch. So, for the price of four Texas size hamburgers plus fries (super-sized) the sign crew came to our rescue.

At the moment another problem confronted us. This cloudy and windy spring day was now threatening rain. For our carpenters to be safe on a steep roof 50 feet up, we would really need calm and dry weather. In prayer we all called on the One who calmed the storm to help us. Just as the sign crew finished wolfing down their burgers and fries, a bright patch of blue appeared overhead. The stiff breeze died down. "We can get this done," the supervisor exclaimed. "Come on, guys, full speed ahead," he ordered in his skipper-like commanding voice.

The man at the controls for the boom operations slowly picked up the 18 foot spire, hoisted it 50 feet up and carefully sat it atop the lantern pinnacle on the peak of the chapel's roof. As soon as the spire was bolted securely in place, the patch of blue in the clouds disappeared. The winds of March returned. Then it began to rain, first softly, then hard.

Back down on the ground, all our workers knew we had witnessed a miracle. The sign supervisor reminded us confidently, "Believe me, you had God's help today, men. No way we could have done this with your spire swaying dangerously in the wind!"

We know we have enjoyed at least a hundred such miracles of divine help.

When we began erecting the walls of the chapel, we were given a small but efficient mobile home to serve as a construction site office. Since our builders did not utilize this dwelling, we lent it to another start-up ministry. Two of Jim Mackey's disciples, Mark and Mary Sorenson, had come out of a background of drug addiction. Their vision now was to develop a residential discipleship program to help young men escape a life of crime and/or addictions. They called it Straight Street. Today they have their own facility at the end of a street called "Straight." But our hilltop was where their first young disciples came for residential training.

Mary is a gifted interior designer. Her operation, Cedar Hill Design Center, is now a thriving, eye-catching business. JoAn and Mary worked together on our chapel's interiors. They labored over colors, flooring, material samples, and fixtures. It was their goal to create in our chapel a welcoming, comfortable living room effect. This was important since we have always been a home cell oriented congregation. As paint contractor, Mark had his young disciples working with him, finishing our walls with craftsman quality work. This required some degree of Mark's careful oversight.

We were extremely busy wrapping up details for the Consecration of the House. In May of '94 we sent out this engraved invitation:

> Giving Glory to God,
> Pastor and Mrs. Robert Summers
> with the Elders and Saints of
> Mountain Creek Community Church
> request the honour of your presence
> at the Consecration of the House
> Sunday, the third of July
> nineteen hundred and ninety=four
> Prayer Mountain
> 5950 Eagle Ford Drive
> Dallas, Texas 75249
>
> "Built upon the foundation of
> Apostles and Prophets
> Jesus Christ Himself the Chief Cornerstone."
> Dinner on the Grounds following

The very last projects were the paving of Prayer Mountain Lane—a huge miraculous gift—and the installation of the church pew furnishings. The lovely benches did not arrive until Thursday afternoon, June 30, less than three days before the dedication service. To speed the two man installation crew along, our men gathered to help unload the trucks.

Friday, July 1, the furniture men assembled the pews and began positioning them according to the pattern. One of our Elders, Michael Trombley, had been in charge of the constant set up and breakdown of chairs during construction. He dropped by to celebrate and to insist: "Nail those suckers down to the floor. I don't want to ever move chairs again!" Those "suckers" are still nailed down.

The day of the Consecration of the House arrived on Sunday, July 3, 1994. We had worked long hours almost every day of June in preparation for this moment. Loving friends and well-wishers from all around the state came to celebrate with us. One count put the size of the overflow crowd to be nearly 500 folk. All the presbytery leaders were there to speak blessings over us.

To God Be the Glory was our opening hymn. Scriptural songs were also woven in with more old hymns like *We Gather Together to Ask the Lord's Blessing.*

JoAn led the chapel choir in Larry Goss' great anthem, *Cornerstone.* Turning to something more formal, but no less beautiful, the choir then sang Brahms' *How Lovely Is Thy Dwelling Place*—the verses of Psalm 84 from *The German Requiem.* Then the choir swung into the familiar rousing *Hallelujah! Chorus* from Handel's *Messiah.*

We consecrated this edifice as a house of prayer with the orations of seven separate prayers led by various church leaders. One of our opening prayers was in Spanish, led by Manuela Diaz, José's widow. She had continued his dream of the Palacio del Rey church on Dallas' Illinois Avenue.

Our pastor, Des Evans, gave the charge. He challenged us from 2 Kings 6. There the sons of the prophets enlarged their meeting house and their dwelling place. These prophetic, visionary people, under the leadership of the prophet Elisha, were eager for enlargement. The Lord helped them. He even sent them miraculous help, such as the floating axe head, in order to get the job done. Des admonished us to be Kingdom builders, to be prophetic in outlook. And be ready for enlargement! He closed with Isaiah 65:24:

And it shall come to pass
That before they call, I will answer;
And while they are yet speaking, I will hear.

After a huge dinner on the grounds, JoAn came home to rest and write in her journal. She wrote of how Pastor Des honored all three generations of the Summers family in that beautiful service, our parents, us, and our son. "Mom and Dad Summers received a standing ovation," she wrote, "for their years of service and faithfulness." She closed by recalling the short and simple encouraging words Pastor John Osteen, founder of Houston's Lakewood Church, once phoned in to us at a very discouraging time: "Bro. Bob, (he always knew me as Bob) the vision is true. And God will bring it to pass!"

And so He has surely done it. Whereof we are glad.

"If you're facing a great difficulty, you need faith.
If you're facing an impossibility, you need a miracle."
-Des Evans

There are three stages in the work of God: impossible, difficult, done.
–J. Hudson Taylor, Missionary to Inland China

"I pray heaven to bestow the best of blessings upon this House,
and all that shall hereafter inhabit it.
May none but honest and wise men ever rule under this roof."
–President John Adams in a note to his wife when they first occupied the White House in 1800. These words are now inscribed on the mantel in the State Dining Room.

CHAPTER THIRTEEN

ALL CREATURES GREAT AND SMALL

"Praise God from whom all blessings flow.
Praise Him all creatures here below."
–from the Doxology Hymn

All things bright and beautiful,
All creatures great and small,
All things wise and wonderful,
The Lord above hath made them all.
–Cecil Frances Alexander (1818-1895) *Hymns for Little Children, 1848*

A lovable chapter in the history of Prayer Mountain is the story of our show dogs. They show up at our gate. They are drop-offs. Abandoned. We call them our "show dogs" because they—well, just show up.

Most will come on up the hill sniffing around for a morsel of food. They often come limping, their fur in shambles, their spirits tattered. We've had all kinds and many different breeds. Purebreds, mutts, and Heinz 57 varieties. Some instinctively knew to follow the scent of humans and come on up the hill. Some have waited long and patiently down at the front gate. There they sit in a woebegone slouch, hoping for that return car ride home which never comes. Others hide themselves in the brush, lost as a hard ball in high weeds. Forsaken in the city. Alone, scared, and hungry.

Over the years our folks have adopted well over a dozen beautiful animals. We've been quite a refuge for those of the tail waggin' ilk. People abandon Man's Best Friend for various selfish reasons. Perhaps a boyfriend splits. Maybe a marriage breaks up. Perhaps a move out-of-state. Or simply the cute puppy soon outgrows their small apartment. Who knows why?

Ol' Saint came to us in late summer of '89. When we first saw him at our front gate, he looked like a giant-sized, way overgrown puppy. He brightened all over from head to tail when we pulled up and stopped our car. He came running to JoAn's small red hatchback sports car. He could peer right into the car window without having to rear up on the door. His eyes searched us over. He was really big. I guessed about 90 pounds. I felt sure he was a juvenile, a still growing youngster. He had that unique Saint

Bernard head that gives the appearance of his wearing a nun's habit. His eyes too were telling. They had a way of penetrating your heart with that look of woeful affection. He looked a bit despondent like a kid who just had someone lick all the red stripes off his candy cane. Besides that, his coat was soaking wet. It had been raining for two or three days. I could see the place in the tall grass next to the gate where he had wallowed down. Obviously he had endured a heartbreaking wait for the return ride which never came back for him. Probably been there two or three days. But now you could see hope in his big face.

Back in the rear hatch compartment of Jo's little car, Ransom, our Cocker/Birddog mix, was energized and agitated. As we piled out of the car, Ransom was complaining about this new development. But the big dog, ignoring him, was truly tailwaggin' happy, as if he were saying, "Hallelujah!" in body language. He was absolutely delighted. I think he was blessed to sense that we were dog people. He came up to nudge his big snout against my hand. This flustered Ransom, but ol' big dog just paid no attention to him. Ransom, I think, had an inflated ego. He always gave the impression that he was bigger than his actual size. Now his bigness was a mere delusion beside this truly big dog.

We scrambled around the locked gate and began hiking up the hill. Our every step was closely dogged by our new friend. Ransom had a habit of breaking away from us to run, flop-eared, through the brush to flush rabbits and quail from their cover. But not today. His energy was consumed by rudely carping at the big dog who heeled closely by our side. Ransom was teed-off. But the big dog was unflappable. He just turned a deaf ear. He had found angels, dog-loving angels—as far as he could tell. He pressed in all the closer to our side.

The more we looked at this huge collarless creature, we began to realize that we had a pure-bred Saint Bernard dog following close to us. He looked young and lean. I suspected he would grow bigger. He wanted to be our friend too. He impressed this upon us.

"What do we do with him, this creature?" I asked JoAn.

Her answer came without a pause. "We can't turn away a saint. We just can't." That was it. On the spot we gave him the obvious name "Saint." We decided to find a way to take him home with us. Since Saint could not recount how he came to abide with us, I will quote from the entry in JoAn's journal for that day:

OUR SAINT, Sept. 15 A saint has entered our lives. Literally. For the past couple of days it has been raining, so we did not go out to the hill. This evening we drove out there in my Charger with Ransom in the back. There, waiting at the gate for us was a beautiful, huge, hungry, sweet, gaunt, yearning-for-a-family Saint Bernard dog. No collar. No ID. Evidently a drop-off. His guardian angel (or St. Francis) must have led him to the Gate Beautiful and told him, "Wait here. They will come soon. They love God's creatures." He had been patiently waiting. There was a place he had wallowed out by the gate, waiting for his family to come find him. What's to do?

You can't turn away a Saint!

After all, we're called to minister to the saints. Smile. Much to Ransom's consternation. But I discovered that Robert had always wanted a St. Bernard dog, ever since the fourth grade. So—we piled him into my little car and brought him home.

Hello, Ol' Saint. Welcome home.

Getting Saint into JoAn's little car for the ride home was somewhat a challenge. He could barely squeeze into the hatch with Ransom. But he was eager to ride with us. Once home we fed him the moral equivalent of a side of beef. He had been practically starving.

Ransom soon made his peace with the second dog. Saint did keep on growing— eventually reaching 147 pounds—none too large for his breed. They made a marvelous, inseparable duo, Saint and Ransom. As watchdogs, Ransom did the watching, Saint did the challenging "Who goes there?" role. When we began to build the chapel on the hill, we would at times leave them on the grounds at night as watchmen. No one stole anything.

On one particular night when it was time to go home, Saint just balked. He could not be coaxed into my pickup truck. Ransom rode home by himself in the truck bed. Saint remained back at the hill. I was a bit put out with Saint.

That same night, foul play came to the mountain. Someone or some gang up to no good cut the lock off our back gate and tried sneaking in the back way. We had thousands of dollars' worth of new windows stacked on the slab, awaiting installation. At that time a night watchman named

Tom was staying on the premises, living in his small makeshift recreation vehicle. His dog awakened him. This small *show dog* named Dipstick was an extremely wire-haired dog. He looked roughly like the movie dog Benji—except, as one of our men described him a bit unkindly, "Benji-on-speed." But Dipstick could bark louder than some big dogs. Outside Tom's vehicle some distance away, shadowy figures began backing their small truck into our construction site.

Just then a great roar came out of the dark, unfinished building. The furtive figures began to shout warnings to one another and scramble for their pickup truck. Roaring down on them in hot pursuit was a hundred forty-seven pound monster dog. According to Tom, Saint chased them out the gate and clear down the back road.

Thankfully when we returned the next morning for Saint, both our big dog and the expensive stack of windows were sitting there on the concrete slab awaiting us. Ol' Saint had a proud and knowing look about him as he sat regally by the windows. Of all dogs, only a Saint Bernard can have that appearance—as wise as a tree full of owls. Tom told us all about the midnight incident. Saint was not at all afraid of the creepy thieves in the night.

In fact, Saint was so big, there was only one thing he feared: thunder. At the first crack of thunder he would run for cover. One time Saint was lying in the backyard in the shade of an early summer day. A thundercloud blew up and boomed out its earsplitting report. Saint panicked and bolted for the house. The patio door was open, but the screen door was fastened shut. Saint ran straight for it, never slowing down. He hit the screen at full speed, tearing right through it. He created a giant-sized Saint Bernard cut out pattern in the screen. It left little doubt which dog had done this. Then worse, he tried hiding under the bed. He was far too large to scoot under it. It was quite a scene, made even more comical by this hyperventilating, frightened, huge beast with his head stuck under our bed.

The children of our congregation adored him. They loved playing with Saint. To them he was a gentle giant. Never ever was he gruff with them. They loved his one canine trick. They could ask him, "Saint, what does a big dog say?" He would answer back with a booming "rrruufff!" An eight or nine year old kid with very thick glasses once begged me to let him climb up on the pickup's big rear bumper to get a close look at

Saint. I let him hop up to be at eye level with Saint. He stared at the dog, absolutely stunned. "Wow! Oh, wow!" he exclaimed. Then he groped for some descriptive word. "That's a—that's a mongous dog!" Did he mean humongous? Whatever he meant, the description stuck. Saint garnered the nickname "Mongous Dog."

Saint's one bad habit was lying stretched out in the middle of the road. He could easily jump the four feet over our backyard gate. After sniffing around our neighbor's yard, he liked to go lie in the street like a sphinx. My neighbor, Doug, would find him in the street posed regally and escort him back through our gate. Doug bought me a teeshirt which read: "You Can Move A Mountain But You Can't Budge A Big Dog." Saint's refusal to budge while posing and reposing in the middle of Prayer Mountain Lane earned him the only newspaper spanking he ever received. He had backed up three or four cars while lying there. He seemed to enjoy bringing the traffic to a halt. He got his bottom busted for that naughty trick. The one time I spanked him he whimpered like a kid. Made me feel bad too.

I often took Ransom and Saint in my pickup truck to Canyon Lake. Usually I traveled the back roads through the countryside. At every stop in small towns, families would gather around to stare and inquire about the big dog. Saint always loved company and seemed to thrive on admiration.

In the midst of our involved struggle to build the chapel on the mountain on a cash basis, I left town for a Memorial Day rest break. I headed for Canyon Lake, exhausted. Because of the warm day, I continued to spray cool water on Saint. The Memorial Day traffic was extremely heavy. I took the Interstate this time. Finally the flow down the highway came to a grinding halt. The Interstate through Austin was now a long, long parking lot. I took a detour and picked my way around the log jam. Radio news and traffic reports described it as a major accident on the freeway.

Finally when I arrived at our small cabin in the woods, I knew Saint was worn down by the long, hot trip. He hopped down out of my Ford Ranger pickup and headed for the spring creek nearby. I proceeded to unload our luggage and open up the house. Perhaps twenty minutes later I looked around and did not see Saint. Ransom was underfoot but Saint was nowhere to be found. So I headed down into the creek bottom. Suddenly what I sighted was the worst possible thing a tired man would find.

Saint was lying still, almost upside down, quite like a giant dead armadillo by the roadside. His eyes had rolled back into his big head. He had either died on the spot or had a stroke. I called out loudly for JoAn to come. I began to splash cold spring water over Saint's still body. I beat on his chest. I began to rebuke death. My heart throbbed. My stomach sickened. Already I was so weary from our busy building effort in Dallas. Now my big dog lay dead at my feet.

JoAn came quickly running and began to pray over Saint. Tears flowed down her cheeks. Long moments passed. Then I thought I detected a pulsing heart again. Yes, I did! Saint began to breathe. He was alive! Finally, with great effort he lifted his big head. He looked up at us with his woeful long face. I continued to bathe him. Then he made a struggling effort to stand up. With my help he did manage to get up on his feet. As I steadied him, he walked back to the house. We let him lie down under a cool air conditioner. He slept an hour or so, breathing deeply and for him, normally. When he woke up he was once again our big hungry dog. We were so amazed and very thankful. The Lord had heard our prayers. Our few days of rest did not include having to bury Ol' Saint.

He lived five more years. When he died, during a thunderstorm of course, J.D. helped me bury him beneath a rock outcropping on the mountain. A Peace Rose still grows and blooms over the big dog's grave. Ransom and we missed him greatly, but soon another beautiful animal entered our lives.

If it were possible to dignify a dog by elevating him to the status of a "noble creature" surely Simon would fit that description. He got his Biblical name when his little old lady owner, observing his virtuous nature, felt he should be christened some worthy name. She named him Simon, after Saint Peter. She then sent this somewhat religious dog to obedience school, her idea of the closest thing to a dog seminary. By the time Simon was five years old, his owner was bound for a nursing home. She was desperate to find him a suitable home. We got the phone call from one of our members, Cathy, who was assisting the lady's move.

"Please trust me on this one," our friend told us. "This is the best dog I've ever seen. He's much too good to be sent to the shelter. I would personally like to keep him, but I've already got two dogs in my small backyard. Can you help me find him a good home?"

JoAn and I thought out loud—about JoAn's recently widowed mom, Eva. JoAn's dad, Jofred, had passed away six months previously. Now Eva was alone. She needed a well-behaved dog. We decided to take a chance on Simon, sight unseen.

"Bring the dog to us, Cathy," I replied. Cathy was really pleased. I could tell she felt strongly about Simon's well-being. Shortly he arrived at our house, wagging his tail. All his worldly goods came with him. His personal soft plaid blanket in sort of a pseudo Scottish argyle woven pattern, his chrome dog dish, and a rubber toy bone which had a tinkling bell inside it. He had already outgrown the toy bone. When I tossed it to him, he had graduated beyond fetching it. He sat dignifiedly instead, offering us a handshake. He was definitely left-handed, we noted. A literal *south paw.*

We kept Simon about two weeks before driving him down to Eva's home in Victoria. He had quickly fit in with us, making a close companion to Ransom. We could tell he was well-trained. We felt good about giving him to Eva, even after he seemed to fit in so well with us. She needed the best dog we could find, well-behaved and gentlemanly.

After savoring a meal of Mom Holder's seafood, we left Simon with her. We later learned that he sat patiently by Eva's front door for nearly an hour after we drove away, awaiting our return.

Seven weeks later Eva called us to come get Simon. She felt she could not make the commitment of time and attention the dog deserved, since she had begun working fulltime. So we went back down to pick up Simon. On our return trip to Dallas, we stopped at a park in Waco to give Simon a chance to hop out and relieve himself at the fire hydrant. He balked. He would not get out of the car. It was suddenly apparent that the dog was thinking this one through. He had been left behind before. He was not going to be a left dog this time. No way! He would just "hold it." He remained unmovable in his back seat position with a "Thank you, I'm good" expression. We drove on back to Dallas.

The arrival back at our home was one big happy moment for Simon. He was a picture of euphoria. He checked out every bush and sniffed profusely the sweet, sweet scent of home. His tail wagged with genuine wholeheartedness. He belonged here. This was it.

He and Ransom explored the backyard creek bottom together. We made Simon a bed, placing his folded blanket in the corner of the garage. Simon chose a different place. He promptly pulled his bedding out close by the back door. There he could observe his people inside, peering through the door's window panels. We were soon Ransom's and his favorite TV show.

Simon was mostly Golden Retriever. He had enough mix in him to keep him from ever qualifying for a Golden Retriever dog show. He was a bit smaller than the typical Golden. But he was really quite handsome, more red than golden in color. Hence he garnered the nickname *Red Dog* by those who could never remember which apostle he was named after. One day we overheard the small Royal Ranger boys who were petting him. Jonathan Hart described him as a "Golden Receiver." Little Sam Frickle told the other boys that Red Dog was actually the "official church dog." He pronounced the "oh fishal dog" with the accent on the first big syllable, *Oh*. Another lad chimed in to declare that Simon was "the best dog on his block," a dubious honor, no doubt. Thus Simon turned out to be a Golden Receiver, the "Oh-fishal church dog," the best dog on his block! All the titles stood uncontested. He did fit in well. Very well.

Every time I drove out to the hilltop in my pickup truck, the dogs excitedly wanted to hop a ride. When there on the mountain, Ransom was more interested in flushing game than was Simon. Ransom happened upon a large creature in the brush and yelped to summons us. He had found a huge Great Horned Owl which was for some reason grounded, unable to fly. He was a magnificent bird. He watched our every move.

We called a bird expert, a falconer who worked with the Dallas Audubon Nature Center. He arrived in half an hour. Upon examination of the big bird, his diagnosis was a dislocated shoulder. The avian expert loaded the great owl into a large cage. "Big owls," he told us, "sometimes hit wire fences when they are diving for a mouse."

A few weeks later this owl had mended and was ready to fly again. He was brought back to our mountain for release. His cage door was opened. At first he just stared at us from his open cage, his surprised eyes as big as saucers. Then he shoved off from his perch, shooting free from the cage. He ascended above our heads in an elliptical circling pattern. He dipped his wings once or twice and soared away into the blue. Free at last!

Ransom thought JoAn was *Fab*. And JoAn knew that Ransom was partial to her. She hung a wall motto on her office at home which read: "My goal in life is to be half as wonderful as my dog thinks I am."

When Ransom grew old and weak, he wanted to stay close to us. I made him a comfortable dog bed. In his last few days, I brought his bed into our bedroom and situated the old dog beside the foot of our bed. One night as JoAn lay on our poster bed reading, suddenly Ransom gathered his strength to reach up and softly nuzzle her hand. Then he lay back down quietly and died. We both wept over him. To us it was more than the passing of a favorite little friend. It was the end of an era. Ransom, in his twelve year life span, had seen us through the pioneering stages of development on the mountain. We buried him below a small rock bluff beside his big buddy, Ol' Saint. Now that Ransom is gone, the wild game on the mountain get much less of a workout. No other dog runs through the woods of Prayer Mountain—barking and yelping all the way. Ransom saw that as his waggish ministry.

To my knowledge Simon never flushed any game, not a single rabbit, nor a quail. He just preferred to heel close at the side of his masters. He loved to walk in the woods. But he never ran off on his sniffing trail like Ransom. He especially loved to follow Mom Summers around when she was working the flower gardens on the hill. She moved more slowly with each passing year. But that did not bother Simon. He was often seen at her side. I think he would have wanted to be of more assistance, no doubt. But dogs have no thumbs and are clumsy with gardening. When Mom would sit down to rest on a shaded park bench, Simon would sit at her feet. She was quite fond of him. She would talk to him in a kind of high pitched, soprano dog Latin, and he loved it. He thought she was the greatest.

Simon consistently displayed undying loyalty and obedience toward us. His finest hour came very early on the morning of New Year's Day, January 1, 2005. I had parked my Ford Ranger pickup truck in our home garage late the evening before. Sometime in the wee hours of the morning, it self-ignited. The truck's cruise control switch contact points remained in closed position, even after the ignition was turned off. The resulting heat spark caused the brake fluid in the master cylinder to flash. By the time I was awakened at 2:02 am, I smelled a burn odor and saw haze in our bedroom. I ran through the house in a quick search to see if we had left the cook range burners on. Nothing. I followed my nose down the hall to the doorway leading to the garage. I opened it just long enough to be hit with intense heat and black smoke. Slamming the door, I ran, picked up the phone, and frantically dialed 911 to report the fire.

Next I hastened to roust JoAn out of bed. We grabbed our robes and fled the house. On my way out, the only item I picked up was my set of keys.

Just as we were fleeing out the front door, our local firefighters were arriving, already quickly summing up the situation. A neighbor had earlier called them. He had been awakened by his dog and had walked over, cell phone in hand, to investigate. The fire team captain ran to assist us, questioning about any other occupants in the house. Then he exclaimed that they needed a key to the garage.

"The fire is there in the garage!" he informed us. We could see that the flames had already shattered the window glass and were now shooting skyward.

I had the key in my hand! I ran with him around to the garage. The metal door was already scorching hot. Quickly we worked together to get the door opened. With his heavy fireman's gloves on his hands, the strong captain managed to pull the door up. We had an inferno in our garage. It look like blazing hell had invaded our sweet home.

The firemen went to work. They were a very coordinated, well-trained team. They pulled hoses all through the house. The fire had burned through a wooden pull down attic ladder. Flames had breached through the ceiling to the wooden joists and rafters. The men cut holes in the ceiling and sprayed high pressure streams up into the attic.

In the resulting melee of crisis intervention, all doors and gates were opened for water hose access. Simon suddenly bolted into the burning house, frantically searching for his masters. Red Dog to the rescue! Seeing this, the fire department captain ran to where we were standing across the street. He inquired if we wanted a rescue team to go in after Simon.

"No, no, no!" I blurted out. "We love that dog, but we're not going to lose a fireman for him!"

After three or four minutes a fireman tapped me on the shoulder. "Look, here comes your buddy," he pointed. There was dear old Simon following his nose toward us. Then he practically bounded into our arms. All souls safe and accounted for! Happy dog.

Standing at our side in the dark were our neighbors, Dr. Jack and Grace Cooper. We were watching the activities from their driveway. Being people of prayer and the Word, they continued praying with us for the house to be saved, and for the firemen's safety as well. Neighbors are never more valuable than when you're hit with a catastrophe.

God heard our cry and answered. Our professional firefighters rallied to save the house itself. Only the attached garage was gutted by the fire. Smoke and water damage was throughout the whole edifice. But the captain, proud of this team told me, "We won this one. We've lost houses before which were this far aflame. Couldn't save them. Five minutes later on this call, we would've lost this one. You were five minutes from a raging conflagration. And by the way, yours is the third pickup truck fire we've fought this year." He then wrapped yellow *Do Not Enter—Fire Department* tape around the burned garage doors and the front entryway.

We packed up a few essential items and moved out for two months. Everything had to go in for cleaning and ozone treatment. All the carpet and drapes and bedding were totally ruined. Our home was completely remodeled and upgraded. Later we treated all our firemen and their families to a tasty seafood dinner. They were our heroes. And Red Dog was glad to finally get back to his yard.

When Mom Summers passed away, Simon kept close to my dad. They slowly walked over the hilltop trails. Both were getting well along in years. Dad passed away just eight months after Mom went home to Glory.

Finally Simon, old and feeble, got to where he could no longer hop up into my Frontier pickup with the other dogs, Lily and Bonnie Bear. He just couldn't make it to the mountain any longer. He died at age 16, full of dog years, having served his generation. We buried the dear "Oh-fishal church dog" on the mountain alongside Saint and Ransom in a grave beneath the blooming Peace rose bush, where the big rock outcrops. He was truly "the best dog on his block," a great "Golden Receiver."

Jo eulogized him in her personal journal:

FAREWELL, NOBLE DOG

Robert called him Red Dog. Jonathan Hart once called him the Golden Receiver. I called him Sweet Simon.

He came into our family in autumn of 1998, a beautiful, healthy animal who had no place to go. His owner had to enter a nursing home and he could not go with her. Cathy Mason called, pleading for me to find him a new family. "He's really a wonderful dog. I can't stand to see him go to a shelter, perhaps to be destroyed." Thank you, Cathy, for your caring heart.

Perhaps he would make a good companion for Mother, I thought, since Daddy went to Heaven in March. So I called and convinced her to try it. However, in the few short days he lived with us before we took him to Victoria, he had already chosen us as his new family. We left him with Mother. As we drove away, he sat staring out the door after us for a long, long time. Breaks my heart even now to think of that poignant longing by this noble dog.

A few short weeks later, Mother called us to come get him. She did not want the added responsibility, and she had not bonded with him. Once again we made the trek across Texas. This time to bring him home. That dog was so happy to see us! He refused to get out of our vehicle even to relieve himself on the long trip back. He was <u>not</u> going to be left behind again.

So he became our dog for the next 11 years. In a long heritage of fine family pets, Simon was the most noble.

He was gentle. He was obedient. He was kind and caring of our other creatures. He trained Lily—by pulling on her ear—whenever she was disobedient or willful. It was Simon who told Lily it was safe to bring her four puppies up the hill. It was Simon who persuaded frightened little abandoned Bonnie to come out of hiding in the tall weeds at the bottom of the hill. It was Simon who watched our home when we were gone. He never growled or raised his voice in anger, except for protection of us.

Whenever Mother came to visit us through the years, she was pleased that he always remembered her and loved her. But his loyalties always lay with Robert and me. Kip, Val, and the grandgirls loved him too.

This year he turned 16—a very old age for a dog. His hearing failed. His eyesight dimmed. His strength ebbed each week. He no longer took great joy in the truck rides to the hill—once the highlight of his days. Finally he chose to stay home altogether, letting Lily and Bonnie romp without him. Age exacted its toll. He slept most of the time. Waking to eat, he wobbled about on splayed, shaky legs.

He never went out to the fish pond as far as I knew. But while we were gone to the hill country, we received a call from Tony. Christina went over to feed our animals and found Simon in the pond—dead. We suppose he followed Lily's scent, not able to see, fell into the water, and had no strength to pull himself out. Tony buried Simon in his favorite blanket, out beside Ransom and Saint. Thank you, Tony.

Simon was such a gift of God to us. He blessed us with loving loyalty through all these years. We miss him.

When I texted Kip, I said, "Simon went to dog heaven today. He was the best behaved dog we ever had." Kip texted back the words of the Brad Paisley song:

"When I get where I'm goin'
There'll be only happy tears…
Yeah, when I get where I'm goin'
Don't cry for me down here." Simon was a good boy!

Yes, he was a good boy. A noble dog. Farewell, Sweet Simon. Thank you for eleven years of undying devotion.

Lily showed up at the mountain right around Christmas time of the year 2000. She was starving and gaunt. What's worse, this pitiful mother dog with a broken chain fastened to a choke chain collar around her neck was nursing four healthy, fluffy, roly-poly puppies. She was too frightened to come on up the hill. So Allen, one of our ministers called upon Red Dog, who was visiting that day, to go along with him to coax her up to the top.

Simon (Red Dog) went along with Allen to the rescue. In a language only canines comprehend, he whispered some reassuring words to the abandoned, woebegone mama dog. So she followed Allen and Red Dog along the lane, the fat puppies in close, pell-mell procession.

At our offices, JoAn found some milk and cereal in the kitchen for the new family. When she dished out the food in a saucepan, the puppies wildly rushed it and squirmed, contending for the pole position at the makeshift trough. Obviously mama dog was hungry. But she backed off to let her wiggly brood gorge on the food. Watching this noble, but ragged dog give way to her pups was too much for JoAn. She was nonplussed. She exclaimed to the animated crowd of food-wolfing puppies, "Get back away, you fat little creatures! Let your mama have some of this food!" She pulled a couple of the fattest pups out of the lineup. She pushed mama dog up to the pan. Only then did the little mother eat, never infringing on her babies.

JoAn knew she had seen something magnanimous in this deferring and caring animal. Her puppies were healthy and well cared for. Yet she was near starvation. We found a large weatherproof box for a makeshift shelter to house the new family. A cold front was due to blow in that night. The furry family could snuggle down in that big box.

The next morning we brought some meaty dog food for the new dog household. We observed that the puppies, now eating soft food, were about ready for weaning. By Christmas we had placed all the dogs into good homes as Christmas puppies. We kept the mother. JoAn named her Lily. She was pretty much white all over—lily white—except for a few golden spots and freckles.

A lady beautician visiting us exclaimed over Lily's white fur in her flat Texas drawl, "It was good of the Lord to brang you such a purty what dog." A what dog! From then on, Lily acquired the nickname "What Dog." We had no idea how beautiful Lily the What Dog would become when she filled out and took on her long winter coat. She became a beautiful, happy animal.

Lily managed to spare me a lot of pain, maybe even saved my life. That summer I was out in the deep woods of the mountain with Red Dog and Lily. (Lily had to learn to stay near me. Red Dog would pull on her ear whenever she was stubborn or disobedient. He was a good trainer.) I was moving through some thick brush in a new unmarked area. I was flagging protected trees with surveyor's red flagging tape, marking the way for J.D. who was directly behind me on a small crawler/bulldozer. We were blazing a new trail. When darkness began to fall upon the forest, J.D. decided to head the dozer back to the tool yard. I waved him goodbye. I intended to flag a few more trees on my way back to the main trail. In my hands I carried limb loppers, big commercial limb loppers with extra long handles. This is an essential trail finding implement, especially in heavy brush.

Suddenly Lily cut in front of me. She often did this. She loved to flush out game. Maybe she was half bird dog. Instantly she halted, five feet away from me. She growled. Her hair stood up on her back. She was braced to attack. In the dense undergrowth, she had come across danger. Whatever it was, it was hidden from my view beneath a small bush.

What would make Lily bristle and growl like that? I took my limb loppers, reached forward, and snipped off the upper half of the bush. Suddenly what I saw sent a shot of adrenalin through my body. A fairly large copperhead snake was coiled under that bush. The deadly viper was distracted by Lily. He was now poised to strike her as soon as she stepped closer. The snake never noticed me. I acted quickly—although I was a bit shaky. Using my big limb loppers, I caught that viper's head in the grip of its cutting scissors. Using all my strength, I snipped its head off. The snake, now headless, writhed momentarily. Then its decapitated form lay still. I trembled as I finally caught my breath. I sighed and thanked God. Angels watching over me! And Lily.

I had been only three or four steps from walking past that small bush. When Lily had sensed danger, she had darted ahead of me. Copperheads never get as large as rattlesnakes, but they are just as deadly. Unlike rattlesnakes, copperheads give no warning. They use the element of surprise and concealment to their advantage. That sneaky snake lay in wait for us. But Lily's nose had warned her. After that snake incident, Lily's value to me while in the wilds was incalculable. Off the charts! Lily was now my hero dog.

I hastened out of the darkening big cedar woods. Next day I brought J.D. and JoAn back to see the dead trophy snake. After this episode, I did not leave home without Lily if I were going to work in the woods. She had earned a lifetime of pickup truck rides.

A lot of good dogs, and a few good cats, have shown up on our mountain. To recall a few: Tuxedo, the well-dressed black and white cat; Bonnie Bear, the little black Chow Chow (the vet said she was off the charts for docile, gentle manners); Zack, the black lab, and Samson, the big German Shepherd. All were adopted by our pet-loving members.

I suppose the friendly environment of Prayer Mountain attracts creatures both domestic and wild, both great and small. We are a wildlife refuge. Besides the castaway pets, we often see bobcats, foxes, and coyotes. The bobcat kittens are cute enough to take home. But we don't dare.

We have never lacked for left dogs. Happily, we have managed to find them all good homes. The animals have been an unforeseen bonus that came with the mountain. Who could have known the abandoned Saints, the Red Dogs, and the *What* Dogs would have brought us all such joy?

Over the years we have learned a lot of enduring lessons from our dogs. People who have big dreams and visions need to remember the one fundamental rule Ol' Saint taught us: *The bigger the dog, the more the fleas!* That's a good proverb to remember. We like big visions, big visions with few problems. But life never works out that way. That certainly has been true of our Prayer Center on the mountain. The bigger the vision for these 100 acres, the more the problems. Yet the result was an exercise of ever increasing faith in God. And He was faithful to help us overcome.

He prayeth best, who loveth best
All things both great and small;
For the dear God who loveth us,
He made and loveth all.
–Samuel Taylor Coleridge,
The Rime of the Ancient Mariner

CHAPTER FOURTEEN

ALL GENERATIONS, ALL NATIONS

This will be written for the generation to come,
that a people yet to be created may praise the Lord.
Psalm 102:18

I am the God of Abraham,
and the God of Isaac,
and the God of Jacob.
Matthew 22:32

It is written, My house shall be called a house of prayer for all nations.
Mark 11:17

Like the fresh, warm breezes of an early spring zephyr, a new breath of renewal was blowing across Texas in January of '95. JoAn and I had come to Austin by special invitation. We were there for a significant prayer and strategy dinner at the Doubletree Inn on the Colorado River. This gathering was a prelude to our new governor's inaugural activities. It was the eve of Inauguration Day for Governor-elect George Bush.

Our incoming governor had requested the presence of many Texas pastors to attend the Capitol ceremonies and join Billy Graham and Franklin Graham in praying for integrity, humility, and harmony in our state government. We were asked to walk up Congress Avenue from the Prayer Breakfast and to pray over the Capitol precincts. A very generous Houston physician joined this call to prayer by offering to pay the expenses of at least three hundred pastors and wives. His heart was to especially assist Hispanic church leaders. In turn, these particular leaders included JoAn and me in their delegation. We had worked closely with *Oracion Explosivo* (Prayer Explosion) which involved many Hispanic pastors and evangelists. They were a spiritual group which prayed arduously for church unity, family values, and national revival.

This was such a far cry difference from the previous governor's inauguration. When the acerbic-tongued Ann Richards was sworn in, the streets of Austin exploded in celebration. Hundreds of homosexual groups from "Act Up" and "Queer Nation" had danced in the streets then. Indecency had ruled the day. Literally.

The evening before Governor Bush's inauguration, JoAn and I were proceeding down the long hotel corridor toward the ballroom for dinner. We turned a corner and came upon a trio of business suited gentlemen who in friendly fashion turned to greet us. To our amazement, we found ourselves face to face with Billy Graham, his son Franklin, and another bishop friend. After cordial introductions, Dr. Graham began to ask us about our ministry in Dallas. We told him about Prayer Mountain. His interest was genuine. We carefully avoided monopolizing his time. Yet this impromptu encounter was certainly engaging. It was completed by a short admonition from Billy Graham. We will never forget his words. "You need to put out a call," he said with simple firmness, "to the Koreans to come help with your vision of Prayer Mountain. They know how to pray."

I assured Dr. Graham we were already involving a congregation of Koreans who were now praying with us. "Yes," I agreed, "they do know how to pray."

The rest of the story in Austin was that Texas went on to enjoy a decade of good government, peace, and prosperity. Even after George W. Bush left to become President of the United States, his home state continued to grow and prosper. And so did we. The prevailing prayers of our Korean friends were a blessing. They would often come to JoAn and me and ask us to teach them how to parent. They explained that they were all descendants of war orphans who had no idea how to train up children. But they know how to get a hold of God. We worked out a parenting school for them. They survived and thrived through the power of prayer.

One of God's greatest blessings is His gift of special people to the church. They touch our lives with kindness and are anointed to bring Christ Jesus and His love to life. Taken together they present us with a ministry medley, revealing the many-sided wonder of the person of Christ. It has been my good fortune for the past 16 years to meet weekly with a diverse group of church leaders in Southern Dallas.

One lesson that has broadened my view of the multicultural church is that differing ethnicities have ministry gifts that are unique to their culture. This is especially true of prayer.

Once when our Southern Dallas ministers' group was praying about the terrible murder rate—especially toward young men—in South Dallas, our orations were almost flat-lining. We started out with mild *Kumbaya* type prayers which seemed to bounce back down from the ceiling. When the turn came for one of the more scrappy African-American pastors to pray, he dropped the gentle, dignified manners. "Guys," he said, "Jesus told us in Matthew 7 to 'ask, seek, and knock.' We've done enough asking and seeking. It's time we start knocking. Not just an easy, friendly knock. It's time for the police knock!"

By the time he belted out the word "PO-lice" he was rapping his knuckles hard on the table. He then got down on his knees and began to pray forcefully and urgently. Seeing that it was a 911 prayer moment, we all got down on our knees and stormed the gates of heaven for the next 15 or 20 minutes. We broke through. Something got moved out of the way between us and the throne of heaven. The crime rate in our city did indeed drop after that event. I have never forgotten that term "police knock." I've used the PO-lice knock with success in a few tough prayer sessions since then.

We need the various ethnicities and their unique energies. In the New Testament there was not a White church, a Black church, nor a Hispanic church. The only distinction among believers was Jew and Gentile. The *ethnos* of the New Testament was a *one new man* wherein all were joined together into one body having *been reconciled through the cross of Christ.*[26] All were members of the household of God, for Christ had abolished in His flesh the enmity between races. We are moving into that unity today in the contemporary church of God. This reconciling of the races in the church is the message I hear from every apostolic and prophetic voice in the country. The time is way overdue.

Beginning about fifteen years ago we began to take on the characteristics of a diverse, multicultural congregation. This reflects the ethnic makeup of the communities around us. About the same time, the Lord brought us Delbra Stevens. She is a beloved woman of prayer. Now a virtual matriarch, she participated years ago as a youth in the South's Civil Rights movement. Delbra's strong influence in the church is in intercession and in rallying compassion ministries for the poor and dispossessed; children and families alike. She is practical. In displaying a natural aptitude toward hard work, she is capable of being tough. It is because she is spiritually clever, not lacking in discernment. No one fools Delbra. She currently directs an outreach store to the needy known as "His Hands Extended." She has made the truth of Proverbs 19:17 a working reality:

He who has pity on the poor lends to the Lord,
And that which he has given He will repay to him.

It is amazing how Mountain Creek Church functions as a family team even though its multicultural congregation has diverse traditions, tastes, and sensitivities. We've learned to discover one another's strong gifts. It is the work of the Holy Spirit to blend these distinctive attributes into one body—without obliterating their unique benefit. "For in fact," Paul teaches us, "the body is not one member but many."[27] Paul then goes on to use the physical body as an example of the need for each diverse member. He makes a case, a plain one at that, for the fact that it is best that the Body is not all a foot—with the gift of walking. Neither is it all a hand—with the gift of grasping. Each member is needed. Each one with its distinctive function. Each with its unique adeptness. "How could we see," he asks, "if all were an ear?"

A multicultural, multigenerational blend makes a church more fun and much more capable of fulfilling its God-called destiny. Each culture, each generation brings something of a unique gift to add into the mix of the House of God.

The scriptures often reference the Lord as being the God of three different generations of patriarchs. He is the God of Abraham, Isaac, and Jacob. He is the God of Abraham, the altar builder and digger of wells. He is also the God of Isaac, the prosperous middle generation who also dug wells and opened up the wells of his father, wells which Abraham's enemies had filled with debris. The Lord is the God of Jacob. Jacob was the cheater who nonetheless desired the eternal blessing of God. He is first to reference the *House of God* in Genesis 28 as the place where he encountered God in a dream. "How awesome is this place," he declared. "This is none other than the gate of heaven and the house of God." He arose to make an altar of a large rock and vowed his vows unto the Lord. He fathered the sons of Israel. Jacob, like Isaac and Abraham, can be remembered by his prayers.

Abraham prayed early in the morning.[28]

Isaac prayed in the evenings.[29]

Jacob met God in dreams of the night. He also wrestled with the Lord through the night.[30]

We still emphasize those three times as best suited for prayer. Prayer meetings held in early mornings will attract mostly the older, early risers. We think of evening prayer meetings as vespers. These meetings are best suited for the middle aged, general assembly attenders. The Isaac generation is generally prosperous because they have good jobs or head up businesses. So they can't stay and pray very late for obvious reasons. The younger praying saints, the college age youth, can take the night watches, tarrying even to the morning watches. They are the Jacob generation. They love to linger in the presence of the Lord. They energetically wrestle through the night until they get a divine response.

There are many times we can walk over the hilltop and hear serious prayer in several different languages. Upon hearing all the intense prayer in foreign languages, a friend once remarked to me, "I can tell you there's probably not a demon within five miles of this place. At least it would sure be uncomfortable for them to come near here."

Jim Cymbala, pastor of New York's well-known congregation Brooklyn Tabernacle, spoke this word to a gathering of us pastors: "Where you find prayer, you find faith. The first act of faith is to reach out, to pray. Faith always reaches out."

It is through prayer that we breathe deeply of the Holy Spirit's power. Prayer builds courage to activate the present and anticipate the future. A praying people look forward to greater days of grace. The Lord always has more in store for His people.

Old folk have an important place here as well. Messiah Jesus was born into an atmosphere of a praying remnant which included the elderly. In fact, every spiritual work of God can be traced to a praying person or persons. Key players in making this inaccessible mountain beautiful and enjoyable by all God-seekers were Lester Paul and Mary Summers, my parents. They came to be known affectionately by the young people as Mom and Dad. We cannot emphasize enough their gift of prayer, their vision, and loving service. Their day here began with Mom sitting at the grand piano in the chapel playing beloved old hymns. Dad Summers would remain at the altar for at least a sweet hour of prayer. They often reminded the Lord of one of their favorite Bible promises, found in Jeremiah 33:3, "Call unto Me, and I will answer you and show you great and mighty things which you do not know." To them this verse was more than a promise. Jeremiah 33:3 was God's own personal phone number, the direct backline to His office.

In a city where the face of Christianity has sometimes been the self-congratulatory showman, Mom and Dad served in the modest and hidden role of intercession. In my mind at least, they were some of the last of the all-time greats. Speaking of the last, up to the end of his 89 years of life, Dad could still be seen walking over the mountain, leaning on his cane, with Red Dog faithfully by his side. He was out for his daily walk and talk with God. Even after his memory faded and he was not always able to recall my name, he well remembered his Lord. He could still pray. Mom and Dad loved this hill. Only Zion's Hill in the heavens held more appeal to them.

A couple of days before Dad's transition to glory, he lay in the hospital in a comatose state. We sang over him his favorite hymns. JoAn sang his beloved special song, *Zion's Hill*. He responded when she came to familiar lines,

Someday beyond the reach of mortal ken,
Someday God only knows just where and when
The wheels of mortal life shall all stand still,
And I shall go to dwell on Zion's Hill.[31]

She was quite surprised to see Dad raise his bony old finger and twirl it to signify the motion of a wheel. Then he pointed upward to some higher ground he could now visualize. It was no longer far away.

In their own way, and at their own speed, Mom and Dad kept busy almost to the end of their lives beautifying the grounds with flower gardens. They planted irises, a host of purple and yellow, all along the fences and walls. These flowers still bloom every spring. Mom called it "piddling." But their activity left us a small legacy. Here and there patches of something bright and beautiful appear to remind us. They planted living things for a future generation. That was their style. Yet their strong suit was prayer. Their most valuable contribution was a holy atmosphere, a lingering residue of the Spirit.

Somewhat like Anna and Simeon in the Gospel of Saint Luke's Christmas narrative, they too were old spiritual warriors in the Temple of the Lord. People who pray together share a treasure that this world and all its wealth cannot afford: the joy of the Lord. This is in fact one of the best reasons why we pray. Real church, praying church, is a delight. Church should be heavenly, not heavy. Jesus said, *My house shall be called a house of prayer.*[32] Jesus' house is never dull. It is delightful and glorious. And awesome.

First of all, there is power in prayer. I beg you not to dismiss this as a pious platitude. It isn't. There are some Christians who are such social activists that they never stop to pray. They are wrong, are they not? Prayer is an indispensable part of the Christian's life and of the church's life. And the church's first duty toward society and its leaders is to pray for them.
–John Stott,
from a sermon published in *Christianity Today,* October 2011.

At our ground-breaking ceremony in 1988, Dad Summers turns the first shovel of dirt.

The hills of southwest Dallas from Prayer Mountain.

Pastor Robert stands behind Leonard Ravenhill and his son David who ministered here in the early years.

The original ranch trail up the mountain.

J. D. Dowd came up from Houston to install the original private water line.

Standing on the site he helped to clear, Kip Summers prays at the chapel's ground breaking in February 1988.

Students gather early to worship.

Dad Summers helps to set up chairs in our tent while the building is being finished.

First service in the unfinished chapel.

Summer camps often include bused-in children from low-income government housing, who fish in our pond.

Winter came early to Prayer Mountain in 1990.

JoAn and Kip enjoy watching the bicycle races.

Ol' Saint loved to lie on Prayer Mountain Lane and stop traffic.

One of the prayer decks overlooking Emerald Lake and Mountain Creek Parkway.

Mom Summers pauses for a rest from her gardening activities, including planting of hundreds of irises.

Dad Summers on his daily walk over the mountain with Red Dog.

The popular western prayer deck looking toward Cedar Hill State Park and the big lake. The view is great.

Sailing Flathead Lake with the Webers (niece and nephew) who head up CBN television operations in Kiev.

Promise Keepers, Coach Bill McCartney and Raleigh Washington came to celebrate the Feast of Tabernacles with Robert and JoAn.

icnics are a common delight on the mountain.

he Mountain Creek Church Choir brings music to the mountain, filling the services with worship.

One of the many miracles of healing: Larry Anderson was dying, in Stage 4 cancer.

Mackenzie, Saint, and Ransom.

The Summit building surrounded by bluebonnets in spring.

Robert and JoAn walking the rampar walls in Old Jerusalem.

Children's music camp musical.

Mountain Creek pond, children's fishing hole.

The front gate is always open on Prayer Mountain Lane.

allas Baptist University students, Chase d Jarrod leading a prayer at Fire on the lountain.

Pastor Des Evans visits the construction site along with David and Leonard Ravenhill and our spiritual son John.

astor Robert hiking in the woods with ed Dog.

Dallas Off-road Bicycle Association and their Texas State Mountain Bike rally attracts hundreds of bikers.

he view of the hills in Autumn from the trail ridge leading to the prayer decks.

The concrete crew lays the foundation of the chapel.

JoAn watches with Ransom and Saint as the buildin is framed up.

Texas State Mountain Bike Rally on Prayer Mountain's Big Cedar Trails.

All the recent mayors of Dallas have visited Prayer Mountain and requested prayer from the Southern Dallas pastors. Here shown is Tom Leppert (white shirt

Christmas party in the Summit.

Music was really big in my life. I was pleased to find in JoAn an experienced musician. I would also discover her proficiency in another favorite area of my studies, Spanish. I had grown up rapping with both Hispanic friends and Spanish-speaking missionary kids. In one of the last night events of the camp, all we youth were hiking up to the top of the hill for a fireside devotional. I glimpsed JoAn's eyes in the light of a full moon as I assisted her up a steep incline on the trail. I was too timid to express what I really wanted to tell her. So I spoke it to her in my best Spanish, "*Tu eres muy linda in la luz de la luna.*" (You are very pretty in the moonlight.) To my astonishment, she quickly turned to face me with eyes wide open. "Muchas gracias, señor," she replied. Stunned, I didn't say a word for a long minute. "You speak Spanish?" I finally broke the silence of my surprise. "Sí, sí. It's a favorite course of mine in college," she answered me.

I moved quickly to meet her parents at a July 4th barbecue at JoAn's home. On our very first date in Houston, I took her to a free concert under the stars in Hermann Park with the Houston Symphony Orchestra playing Von Suppe, Bizet, and Tchaikovsky. A romantic and inexpensive evening to be sure. Later on, as young married teachers on a tight budget, we nonetheless managed to hold season tickets to the Houston Symphony.

So it would naturally follow that when we began to develop Prayer Mountain we would build a music program into the work. Priestly worship is essential to effective prayer. JoAn directed the music ministry. We sang various kinds of music, from Brahms to Brooklyn Tabernacle. We soon learned the blended multicultural style of the music of Carol Cymbala's Brooklyn Tabernacle Choir usually had the biggest appeal to our mixed audience. Also the arrangements of J. Daniel Smith, leader of the well-known Bethesda Church Choir in Fort Worth, are favorites.

Although priestly choirs played a major role in Solomon's Temple, they have become a rarity in the contemporary church scene. This may be because many choirs do not truly worship. Emphasis has been placed on musical proficiency rather than on ministry. Singers' faces are often buried in sheet music. Not much of an inspiration for sure. JoAn has long been impressed that the Brooklyn Tabernacle Choir prayerfully ministers instead of performs. As well they should. Music ministry ranks with pulpit ministry in Biblical importance. It needs to be treated as such. The sound of heaven opens hearts to hear the Word of heaven. A good choir requires good leadership, plus a lot of prayer, practice and proper pieces to sing in a way that will truly minister. It involves hard work. It also calls for fun and fellowship. Choir alumni from Christ for the Nations Institute still fondly recall the fun they had in that school's choir—which JoAn began. The same is true for a great worship service.

It is a gift to know the difference between just making music and truly worshipping. Granted, some musicians may not know the difference. But a great worship band understands that its role is a *holy* calling. To worship God in a way that inspires others to follow is the key thing. In a multigenerational spiritual family there will naturally be tension over style, contemporary sounds, and even volume settings. Blended worship seeks to mix the different generational preferences in a way that is rewarding to all. The Holy Spirit needs to be present in every decision the worship team makes. *Where the Spirit of the Lord is, there is liberty.*[33] Worship is absolutely vital to prayer breakthroughs and the Believer's victory. Worship teams should be more prayerful over their selected praise line up. Unfortunately, many praise bands will pray for only four or five minutes. They then will struggle for an hour and a half in rehearsal trying to perfect their musical sound style. The preparation of the musician's heart is far more important than the preparation of the music.

Unfortunately many praise bands have discarded the great old hymns of the faith. Perhaps they cannot easily blend them into their upbeat contemporary tempos. Here is a Biblical response: A fellow pastor, Mike Massa, is also a teacher of worship leaders at Christ for the Nations Institute. He explains that while retaining the old songs we should be singing new ones. Many great scriptural songs celebrated a victory. In the Psalms and in Isaiah, we find seven times the admonishment to "sing a new song." Most of those new songs were in celebration of a new victory or great deliverance. A good example is in Exodus 15 where Miriam's song is recorded. Israel had just experienced a new deliverance and witnessed an awesome, lopsided victory. The people had just watched God work in their behalf. "He has triumphed gloriously," they happily sang, "the horse and rider He has thrown into the sea."[34] This was a new moment. The breakthrough called for a new song. We sing fresh songs because we have a new breakthrough.

Mike is right on. This is also why we keep some of the great classic hymns. They represent the epic struggles of their times and subsequent victories. Read the stories behind the hymns. Invariably you will find a heroic, costly win for the Kingdom of God. A timeless hymn was written in celebration for this triumph.

Worship music began to change significantly back in the Jesus Movement era. Singing was no longer confined to the printed hymnal. Nor was the song's page number happily announced by a song leader with his broadly swinging hand marking the meter. New songs were projected on overhead screens. A couple of guitars and an electronic keyboard replaced the central role of the organ in church music. The praise band was birthed. New emerging, younger congregations desired to worship. Musical worship became more than a part in the service featuring two or three songs. Young congregations wanted praise, rejoicing, celebration, and ultimately worship. This movement transformed the way we do music in the church. The emphasis moved from musical talent to ministry to the Lord.

The concept of the worship leader emerged. The worship leader was more than a skilled musician. People hungry for God wanted more than cool notes. They wanted the heart of worship. The worship leader was in many cases a worshipper whose main interest was not merely singing but in ministering to the Lord.

Spiritual leaders saw in this new form of worship ministry a similarity to King David's royal courts of praise. They quoted Amos 9:11 in reference to God restoring psalm singers and priestly choirs:

On that day I will raise up the tabernacle of David, which has fallen down
And repair its damages;
I will raise up its ruins
And rebuild it as in the days of old.

The prophecy of Amos links this promise to *all the Gentiles who are called by My Name.* The theme that high praise is essential for spiritual warfare is a constant concept in the Word.

Aaron's sons were some of the earliest worship leaders in the Old Testament. They had the responsibilities of offering up incense unto the Lord every morning and evening.[35] They also offered up incense on many other occasions. The sweet savor bespoke an aromatic offering, a type of spiritual worship. With time, the old priests smelled of the incense offering. The smell of sweet fragrance permeated their very being, especially their linen garments and hair. You could smell them when they entered a crowded room. They had been at the altar of incense, before the Presence of Almighty God, just a step outside the veil.

A worship leader must *smell* like he or she has been just one step beyond the veil of the Holy of Holies. He must *smell* like worship, like he has just been at the altar in the Holy of Holies. There is a great hunger in the land for true worship, for the sound of heaven. The Lord God himself seeks those who will worship Him in Spirit and in truth.[36] Heaven is filled with this kind of moving worship ministry.[37] The Lord loves praise. He Himself is a singer—in the words of Zephaniah the prophet, "The Lord God is with you. He will rejoice over you with singing."[38] Our singing should then harmonize with the sound of heaven. The songs we sing should glorify the Lord in a scriptural manner and take us into the Presence.

We well remember the first time we heard a truly God-given, anointed new song. (Mercifully, I have forgotten a lot of lesser qualified stuff that passed for praise.) I have never forgotten the moment I heard an anointed new song. Folk who remember the Jesus Movement still miss all those scriptural songs right out of the "King James Hymnbook." Those anthems, such as Revelation 4:11, *Thou Art Worthy*, were popular during that movement. In this same category were worship psalms such as *There is None Holy as the Lord* and *As the Deer*. Simply scripture text.

The Bible heroes show us how true spiritual worship is essential to victorious Christian living. Worship is an affirmation of one's belief. It takes God's Word as absolutely trustworthy. It is an act of believing in the character of the Lord and His established power and glory. It is more than singing. It is spiritual warfare, recognizing *the battle is not yours but the Lord's*.[39] Because worship removes doubts and fears, it prepares us to do battle with spiritual darkness. True worship is an act of faith.

An excellent model for a worshipping congregation is the victory God gave King Jehoshaphat. It is recorded in 2 Chronicles 19 and 20. King Jehoshaphat had just brought reforms to Judah. He had torn down the wooden idols which had occupied the high places of the land. He prepared his heart to seek God. He appointed some of the key spiritual "fathers of Israel" to serve for judgment commanding them to "act in the fear of the Lord, faithfully with a loyal heart."

Then the enemy struck back. Forces from Moab, Ammon, and Syria allied themselves against him, a virtual axis of evil bent on destroying Judah. In the words of the king's messenger: "A great multitude is coming against you."

Jehoshaphat, in the Chronicles' word, "feared, and set himself to seek the Lord, and proclaimed a fast throughout all Judah." The congregations in the land "gathered together to ask help from the Lord." Jehoshaphat then prayed a humble but heroic prayer.

His prayer was answered by the Lord's prophet who brought heavenly encouragement. "You will not need to fight in this battle. Position yourselves, stand still and see the salvation of the Lord, who is with you, O Judah and Jerusalem! Do not fear or be dismayed, tomorrow go out against them, for the Lord is with you."

Jehoshaphat bowed with his face on the ground. The people humbly fell on their faces and worshipped. The king was counseled to send out those singers appointed to sing to the Lord, "who should praise the beauty of holiness." Thus the choir was sent out before the army, saying, "Praise the Lord, for His mercy endures forever." When they "began to sing and to praise," the Lord "set ambushes against the people of Ammon, Moab, and Mount Seir."

The enemy camp, in their confusion and conflict, turned on one another. They literally destroyed one another. No one would escape. When Judah's forces came to their camp in the wilderness, they found no survivors. What the king and his forces found was an abundance of valuables and massive spoils of war. They would be gathering and inventorying for days the material left on the battlefield.

They returned to a victory celebration of rejoicing in Jerusalem. God had wrought a great victory for His people. Those heroic episodes in the Old Testament are recorded for examples, and *they were written for our admonition, upon whom the ends of the ages have come.*[40]

Back in 1997 we faced a major predicament here on Prayer Mountain. The Dallas Fire Department (DFD) informed us we would not be issued any more building permits until we resolved our water supply problem. Due to the 120 foot rise in elevation and the 1200 foot length of our private waterline, we had insufficient water volume and pressure to safeguard our structures from fire. The DFD were super nice guys but the Chief was firm in the demand for sufficient water to fight a fire. Little knowing that all this was the plan of God, we felt the pressure. We were quickly growing. We needed to build more facilities, desperately.

To solve the problem, we began dealing with a group of German investors who owned the almost 67 acre tract next door to us. A City of Dallas water utilities eight inch water main served that large tract of land. In 1996 we had been offered that property for the overrated price of $600,000. Now only a year later we were being given the option of "making any reasonable offer." After prayer, JoAn was given the number of $99,000 as she felt the Lord spoke to her spirit. That was our offer, even though I had thought we ought to offer at least $100,000. Amazingly they responded positively to the $99,000 offer. It was a super bargain. We were thrilled.

Somehow the same Mr. Pearce who formerly was sales director of the now bankrupt and reorganized land company heard of this deal. He quickly ran in under our offer with his own hastily assembled financial backing. He offered half again more than we offered. Our deal seemed to be off, as we were not able to raise the bid.

I shared this with the church, asking them to pray for a favorable solution. That very week, the choir prayed about this matter after our practice. Valerie, one of our altos, spoke up and reminded us of the story of Jehoshaphat's decisive order to send out the choir ahead of the army *to sing and praise the Lord.* In one accord, the whole choir became enthused about actually singing praises over the property and our predicament.

The night was dark. In fact it was a damp, foggy winter night. Using car headlights and flashlights, we improvised a spiritual task force to enter the property by crawling through the barbed wire fence. We sang victory songs and prayed prayers of faith. That land was declared to be the property of the Kingdom of God.

Later, a brother and fellow pastor friend Robert Hogan, visiting from Houston, admonished me to place the Bible, the Word of God on that property. Some folks chuckled. But we were desperate and glad to try it. I can still show you the fork in a large double elm tree where we placed the Word of God. The elements of weather eventually consumed the Word.

The attorneys, who were agents for the German investors, notified us that their investor group had held a parley. They decided in favor of closing the deal with the church and dismissing Mr. Pearce's offer. We bought 66.5 acres of prime wooded hilltop property in Dallas (with views!) for the unheard of price of $99,000. When people ask how we did it, I reply, "We sent out the choir to sing and praise the Lord." Then God gave us the miracle.

We later learned that this beautiful property was the last of a portfolio of ten significant bankrupt properties this group had bought in sealed bids to the Federal Deposit Insurance Corporation. This was the one remaining piece they could not liquidate. As a favor for us, they carried the financed note for a one year payout. We surveyed and engineered a twelve lot Dallas plat which had city street frontage. We quickly sold every lot, paying off the due balance early. There was enough money left over to engineer our city water main and to begin its installation. To God be the glory.

The water main was completed in the year 2000, in time for us to occupy our new Praise Chapel. This is home to the Mountain Creek Choir, those singers who helped us achieve a breakthrough for the Kingdom of God that dark and foggy night in 1997. They sang praises in the damp, dark woods and God gave us the victory.

There was only one problem with this beautiful hilltop land. It had belonged to one of America's biggest homebuilders, Centennial Homes. Next door to this same property, Centennial had started a development on a large scale, a 500 home neighborhood. They had deployed a vast army of excavators and giant earth scrapers. They knocked down a good-sized knoll in the project's center and dumped all that spoil of rock and dirt onto a field in that adjoining 67 acre tract. Unfortunately, they went bankrupt in the housing and real estate bust which hit Texas in 1990. That left a million yards of rock and debris sitting in huge piles on that land next door to us. No buyer wanted to purchase this property in such poor condition. After we bought the property, J.D. was able to smooth and sculpt the big spoil mounds with a bulldozer. The terrain now looks like a park or golf course.

If the Mountain Could Speak

Thanks to our friends at the Dallas Fire Department, we were forced into one of the best moves we have ever made. Almost 67 acres in Southwest Dallas, only miles from everything important in the DFW Metroplex—all for $99,000. It was a God thing! Absolutely!

Sing unto Him a new song; play skillfully with a shout of joy. For the word of the Lord is right; and all His works are done in truth.
Psalm 33:3,4

"Music is a part of our history. It is an expression of who we are and the times we've known, our highs, our lows, and so much that we love. Take away American music from the American story and you take away a good part of the soul of the story."
The historian and Pulitzer Prize-winning author David McCullough from *In the Dark Streets Shineth,* Shadow Mountain Press

CHAPTER SIXTEEN

PULLING DOWN STRONGHOLDS

For their rock is not like our Rock.
Deuteronomy 32:31

By the word of truth, by the power of God,
by the armor of righteousness on the right hand and on the left.
2 Corinthians 6:7

For the weapons of our warfare are not carnal
but mighty in God for pulling down strongholds.
2 Corinthians 10:4

When we finally occupied our hilltop in Southwest Dallas, we felt a dream had come true. But it also turned out to be a real challenge. The attractive hilly country here was an enigma, even puzzling the Dallas civic experts. While the greater Dallas area was experiencing a boom in growth, there was almost no sign of prosperous expansion here. It was as if this region lay bound under a curse.

Posh new upscale development was visible county wide, from far out suburbs to downtown. The construction crane, people joked, was now the state bird of Texas. Sprawling new shopping malls were opening almost yearly. Big box discount stores were everywhere present. High styled custom homes, schools, megachurch campuses, hotels, restaurants, business parks and strip shopping centers were being constructed at a dizzying pace. But not out here. The lack of growth was contrasted sharply with the rest of the Metroplex. Our area was still an isolated wilderness, populated by coyotes and bobcats.

True, the large community development company was now moving mountains of dirt to install miles of buried underground infrastructure. A couple of existing rough settlements were finally vacated. They were up for demolition. That small neighborhood, nicknamed *Little Appalachia*, consisted of only a few shotgun dwellings. It is not an exaggeration to note that the poor creatures who occupied that area all seemed to have an affinity for a littered landscape. They refused to give up on busted ice boxes and beat-up old cars jacked up on cinder blocks, cars that long ago had morphed into shrines of mechanical breakdown. The cult of missing wheels and raised hoods hung out in this place known as Mesquite Flats. Their junky yards also featured loose chickens scratching about, maybe a sow and her small shoats rummaging through trash, and even a goat straining at his chain fastened to the front yard water spigot. Further despoiling the countryside just down the road past an illegal dump site were several small wrecking yards. Cyclone fences and junk yard hounds added to the apocalyptic look. Such was the picture at old, worn-out Florina Road where it crossed Camp Wisdom Road. The back road intersection was as rough as a washboard.

Standing here, you would never know that just over 15 miles to the northeast was the gilded front door of world famous, high fashion Neiman-Marcus at 1201 Main Street in downtown Dallas. Nor would you guess— except for jet liners flying overhead—that one of the world's greatest airports, Dallas/Fort Worth International, was even closer. This otherwise beautiful land, just over a fifteen minute drive from Six Flags Family Park and the Rangers Ball Park, lay totally untouched by wealth's progress.

We would have been ignorant concerning spiritual things and wholly lacking in discernment not to realize something was obviously hindering, something was wrong out here. We thought we had entered our Promised Land. It was not exactly the land of milk and honey. Good fortune had shunned this area. A pall, a dark and heavy covering seemed to be cast over it. We felt we were entering enemy territory. We would have to face our giants. The witches who had held coven meetings on this hilltop (we later learned their identity and deeds) had perhaps locked down this area under misery's curse. Still we encouraged each other in the word of faith. We were determined *to go in to possess the land which the Lord your God is giving you to possess.*[41] We were young and naïve. The devil and his dark realm of demons fought back furiously. Our first three years here on the mountain were times of constant spiritual warfare. Every sordid shot and low blow were aimed at us. We suffered through plots of betrayal, schisms that attacked our unity, and the routine sabotaging of our plans. Divide and conquer was the enemy's ploy. He scored points against us. We *fought beasts* as it were. Yet an emerging core of our congregation remained unmoved and prayerful. Together we survived every low blow. We were often "knocked down" but not "knocked out" as Paul victoriously announced the outcome of his good fight.[42]

We must have moved something in the heavenly realm. In the end, we won the fight. Gone today are the shacks, the dumps, and junkyards. We have linked arms with other emerging ministries here in bringing hope through the Gospel's liberating truth. The region has been truly transformed. Florina Road, once a pot-holed Poverty Lane of sorts, is long gone. I was privileged to serve on a civic committee along with Dr. Gary Cook, President of Dallas Baptist University, Nat Tate, Pastor of Urban Development of Dallas Potter's House Ministries, and a host of other local and state officials in overseeing the extending of Mountain Creek Parkway. It replaced old Florina Road. Actually, we dropped the name Florina because no one really knew just who or where was "Florina." It was good riddance. In place of old Florina is a wide, brightly lighted, divided parkway of four and six lanes. It is now a busy thoroughfare, one of the prettiest in North Texas.

Mountain Creek Community is now a beautiful thriving neighborhood of winding, tree lined drives, new libraries, schools, churches, universities, and parks. Up the street is the new Dallas/Fort Worth National Cemetery for veterans. Lakes and nature trails abound. Just over the hill from us is the new Dogwood Canyon Audubon Nature Center. A booming business park with office centers and warehouses lies a couple of miles north of our mountain. We are also three miles from the unique new Uptown Mall in Cedar Hill. That city has become a prime example of city transformation, inspired by the coming together of civic and spiritual leaders. They have brought their community into a united force to heal the social ills of their town.

The amazing news is that Southwestern Dallas County has recently been discovered to be sitting atop the eastern edge of the Barnett Shale Gas Basin. This vast petroleum basin, lying a mile deep under our hills, has now become one of the largest natural gas producing fields in the United States. Aubrey K. McClendon, CEO of Chesapeake Energy, the largest player in gas production in the nation, reports, "Discovered in the 1990's, the Barnett is the granddaddy of all shale plays. Chesapeake acquired its first assets in the Barnett in 2001, but did not fully appreciate the potential significance until early 2004."[43] Chesapeake Energy has 24 active drilling rigs working, many within view from our hilltop. It is only one of many companies pursuing the gas and oil of the Barnett Basin. Only ten years ago no one really knew the potential of this find. Personally I believe the Lord just hid this treasure, saving it for a time such as ours.

There is a photograph in my study which more than anything else depicts the power of prayer and the Lord's people gaining victory over this area's curse of poverty. The photo shows me in the president's office of a major drilling firm. I am accompanied by Tony Price, one of our elders, and John W. Price, a fellow pastor. A cashier's check, a bountiful settlement which was the signing bonus on the minerals lease of Prayer Mountain, is being handed to me. The money came none too soon. We were well over half finished building the Summit, a beautiful mountain lodge styled fellowship hall, when we ran out of funds.

This sometimes happens when you are building on cash. Everyone has given and given, prayers have been prayed, the saints have labored—and still your cash is used up. As soon as I got the check, I telephoned JoAn who was participating in a Music Conference at New York's Brooklyn Tabernacle. "We can now finish the Summit!" I announced. "And we can install that stainless steel kitchen!" The Summit was completed, debt free, and dedicated in 2006. Just in time for the annual Christmas Party. A marvelous gift to the church.

How in the world did we get to this place of blessing? How did we go from an isolated, derelict mule ranch in a dirt poor area to hit pay dirt? The answer is God. The Lord responds to the prayers of His children, especially when they pray the Word of God. We have not tried to pull down strongholds all by ourselves. We have teamed up with other congregations who have prevailed in prayer with us. They have been partners in our struggle. Together we have discovered the life changing resources of the Spirit's power to transform our neighborhoods. We still have much work to do. But we are no longer alone.

"We are now living in the age of the Holy Spirit. We will never be able to accomplish our mission successfully in this world if we don't recognize His work."
–Dr. David Yong-gi Cho,
Korean pastor who built the world's largest Christian church in war torn South Korea, from *The Fourth Dimension, Vol. II*

CHAPTER SEVENTEEN

MADE FOR BATTLE

For You have armed me with strength for the battle; ...
You have also given me the necks of my enemies.
Psalm 18:39-40

And when the fight is fierce, the warfare long
Steals on the ear the distant triumph song
And hearts are brave again, and arms are strong.
(From the hymn "For All the Saints" by William How)

Invariably where daring faith is struggling to advance against hopeless odds,
there is God sending "help from the sanctuary."
–A.W. Tozer, *Paths to Power*

On the mountain we are blessed to be both a popular vantage point and a friendly family park. From our prayer decks the outlook is sweeping. The view of the metroplex extends to faraway landmarks, some 25 to 30 miles distant. Fifteen miles of expertly developed mountain bike trails crisscross through the woods and over the hills. We've had more fun here than most people know. Joy has been our banner, flown high over this mountain. Sure we have had our trials and pressure points. But this hill could just as well be festooned with banners of victory.

Like a thread running through the woven tapestry-like depictions of every episode here is the theme of battle. It links it all together. The spiritual warfare seems to indicate this bit of high ground overlooking Dallas and Fort Worth has far more strategic value than we have known. Principalities and powers of darkness have often been in pitched battle with us for possession and control of this effective station of prayer. *But thanks be to God, who gives us the victory through our Lord Jesus Christ!*[44] He who has never lost a battle fights for us.

Back when I was just a schoolboy, the privilege of playing on a great battleship was one of my chief delights. Our family home was on the Houston Ship Channel's North Shore. We were not far from the old decommissioned *Battleship USS Texas*. It was moored in a slip off the channel at San Jacinto Battleground State Park—in the shadow of the 567 foot tall San Jacinto Monument. The towering obelisk topped with a lone star marks the site where Texans won their independence from Mexico.

If the Mountain Could Speak

In 1836, Sam Houston's ragtag small army decisively defeated the large elite force of the dictatorial Generalissimo Antonio Lopez de Santa Anna. Ever the cruel dictator, despised and feared by his own Mexican countrymen, Santa Anna made an epic blunder at the Alamo. He ordered no prisoners to be taken alive. Davy Crockett, William Travis, Jim Bowie, Jacob Darst (of the Gonzales *Come and Take It!* flag fame) and about 180 other Texan freedom fighters perished in the one-sided fight. He then ordered the massacre of hundreds of unarmed Texans who surrendered at Goliad. They were marched out of town and shot! Sam Houston's small army alone was left to stand up to Santa Anna's vicious advance across Texas. Following what appeared to be the Texans' long retreat, Houston's army cornered Santa Anna's forces at San Jacinto. They caught the general's army nodding in an afternoon siesta. With cries of "Remember the Alamo" the enraged Texans fell upon the surprised foe. The battle lasted only 18 minutes. Santa Anna's routed forces fled in panic and disarray. The despotic general was captured and brought before Sam Houston. His overwhelming defeat and quick surrender secured freedom and independence for Texas.

From time to time our family picnicked at the Battleground state park. As a 12 year old boy I could purchase a snow cone, cross the long gangway to board the big gray warship docked there. Its many ladders and companionways led to all kinds of intriguing places. I could actually crawl up inside its massive gun turrets. Big guns on the *Texas* had fourteen inch bore long barrels capable of lobbing an explosive shell over twenty miles. The ship literally bristled with cannon and antiaircraft weaponry. In make-believe, I could be an ace gunner. And up on the bridge, I could command the great vessel itself. I was the dauntless captain, the determined skipper, relentless in his pursuit of evildoers and various malevolent enemy fleets. Ordering general quarters to battle stations at some crucial naval battle was a familiar function for me. Midway, Iwo Jima, and Okinawa, you name it. Cap'n Bobby was commanding the bridge. Full speed ahead!

Battleship Texas was one of the last of the old giant Dreadnaught (New York Class) warships. The name *Dreadnaught* implied that America had *naught to dread* as long as these ships plied the seas defending her freedom. The old ship was retired to Houston after World War II.

Years later, I visited with friends the very site where the *Texas* saw her last real combat action. We walked the sandy beaches of the Normandy Coast of France. The sheer chalk cliffs still bear witness to the fact that this was once the scene of horrendous combat. They are lined with scores of weathered, deserted Nazi bulwarks and concrete pillboxes—never dismantled. The beach is lovely today but still known for its wartime code name, *Omaha*. The longest day of World War II was fought here in Operation Overlord, but commonly called "D-Day."

Prior to the D-Day landing of the Allied forces in France, many hours before the American amphibious assault on the beaches, the *USS Texas* was there to soften the enemy defenses with her destructive big guns. She fired everything she had. That naval action no doubt saved the lives of many American GI foot soldiers who would storm ashore, June 6, 1944.

Those who did make it to the beach faced fierce enemy fire. The bigger challenge was to cross the beach and make that outrageously frantic climb up the sheer cliffs. There the Army Rangers had to compete for their lives and for every foot of ground upward, locked in mortal combat with their dug-in German defenders. How they managed to make it to the top, I will never know.

Many of them did not make it. At the nearby American National Cemetery overlooking the beach (at Colleville-sur-Mer) we walked with friends softly through the serene burial grounds. It was a misty and melancholy evening. We strolled among the manicured graves of thousands of American soldier boys, their resting place marked by white crosses, row on row as far as eye could see. Here and there appeared stars of David where the sons of Jacob lay at rest. The solemn atmosphere was at once dignified and hallowed, a martyr's memorial, sanctified with the blood of sacrifice. Here lay the first in the charge, heroes who knew no retreat.

Stiff headwinds blowing in off the white-capped sea seemed to compose a dirge of wind soughs singing through the swaying green branches of maritime pines. If you listened in the whispering breeze, you might hear the hushed and tear-filled sound of a million goodbyes. Goodbye to faithful men and boys who will never come home again. Here they lie as a testimony to the price of freedom. Though dead they still speak:

"If ye break faith with us who die

We shall not sleep."[45]

The serenity of the evening was broken by the bugle, sounding the sad strains of *Taps*. It announced the end of the day, the curfew of the cemetery: *Day is done, gone the sun*. We could not help but weep unashamedly. We departed those honored dead with a salute and a prayer. Our souls were moved beyond words.

Back in the automobile, we dried our tears. Sacrifice to us was no longer a mere word, an abstract idea. Those fallen GIs knew the anguish of the ultimate price paid. Because they "gave the last full measure of devotion," Europe was freed from the death grip of Nazism. Today Frenchmen speak French instead of German. Paris did not burn. And because our boys landed in France a remnant of the House of Israel survived. The Holocaust was finally extinguished. Israel was reborn shortly after the fall of Hitler's Third Reich.

I came away from Normandy beach with a life-changing revelation. It dawned upon me that the ol' *Battleship Texas* was not built as a playground for snow cone slurping boys. It was made for battle! It was a ship for brave sailors, men of the Greatest Generation. Those men who fought and won victory at sea saved democracy and freedom. More than sixty years later, we still bask in the triumph of those fighters.

And sixty years ago, A. W. Tozer, one of the church's finest voices, posed the sobering question to the church: "Were we created to be a playground or a battleground?"[46]

Was the Christian church made for battle or for play, a mere entertainment venue? Is this a game we face today? Make-believe warfare or a real spiritual struggle with dark forces in heavenly realms? Sure, faith should be fun. Even joyful. But faith is also a fight, a good fight. The Word of God says more about participating in holy living than it says about fun. The powerful Scottish missionary, Robert McCheyne proclaimed, "A holy man is an awesome weapon in the hands of the Lord." We all need to remember we are at war. We live in a war zone. So a great church service is not just about fun. It is all about winning the fight over an enemy who specializes in killing, stealing, and destroying. We are not living in a *que sera sera* existence. We contend prayerfully for God's will to be done. We have to wrestle for the victor's crown. We have a ruthless adversary. Evil exists.

We can experience the victorious joy of defeating satanic strongholds. The Lord is on our side!

We may take for granted the liberty we have in our musical, upbeat church services. But remember, someone has paid the price for our freedom. Even in the church, a praying remnant must wrestle, and at times be locked in fierce spiritual combat with opposing forces of darkness. Christ Jesus our Lord won the victory for the saints at Calvary's cross. But we who overcome by faith must appropriate the power of His victorious Name. Every thriving expression of the church, the body of Christ, must have an effective prayer ministry. Otherwise there is no power of the Spirit present to heal, to deliver, to set captives free. *Where the Spirit of the Lord is, there is liberty.*[47]

More often than not, the praying people in a congregation are like Gideon's 300 man army. The numbers get reduced until only the few fighters remain. Everyone else goes home. Yet God has always had a faithful remnant who take a stand declaring, "It may be that the Lord will work for us. For nothing restrains the Lord from saving by many or by few."[48] The power of *two or more* in agreement is awesome.[49]

Prayer warriors know the above principle. It is true, nothing keeps the Lord from saving by many or few. But someone has to take a stand. Someone has to lead the charge. Thank God for the remnant in the history of the Christian Church who set themselves in prayer and fasting, and declared, "Not on my watch!" They refused to back down or let it go. And God gave the victory. Leonard Ravenhill, the praying revivalist, used to tell us younger men, "The Book of Acts is not about sanctification. It's about participation. That is why it is called the Acts of the Apostles!" Christian life is all about action. It's about duty and involvement.

We are called to be something more than folk who gather on Sunday morning in beautiful buildings or imposing, important looking edifices. We are called to be spiritual warriors. Christian soldiers. We fight, *not as one who beats the air.*[50] In prayer we take dead aim at the rulers of this present darkness. This is why I love to pray with my Korean friends. They are not afraid to challenge headlong the powers of evil. Here is a caution: prayer is not just about words. As A.W. Tozer warns, "We settle for words in religion because deeds are too costly."[51]

I recall a lesson from the days of the old Communist "Evil Empire" in East Europe. It was in the summer of 1989. JoAn and I were far out in Central Poland in a bucolic little village. We were somewhere between Leszno and Posnan, ministering a semi-secret family Bible Camp. The saints had received governmental authorization to refinish an abandoned ancient estate house in the village of Zeleszno. They were laboring without funds to create a retreat center. The heat of August was severe that summer. Even hotter under their tent of meeting, it was almost unbearable.

JoAn and I had been invited as guests to stay in the home of the local commissar, who was himself an excellent Polish farmer. We were surrounded by pigs, cows, ducks (a pond was close by) and chickens. And millions of flies. We Americans were the biggest diversion to come to this leader's village. He spoke no English. We knew only a few Polish words like "Good-day," "Thanks," "Yes," and "No." And of course "strawberry jam." I think his little village was the strawberry capital of Poland. And that tasted wonderful atop *lodi* (ice cream) if you could get any. All the other food was watery-thin soup and fatty polish sausage.

As was my habit, I arose early to go out to pray. Passing through the tiny courtyard next to the barnyard, I slipped out to Zeleszno pond to find a secluded mott of trees. My prayers there were hearty and a bit desperate. Our travel guide who drove us there had dropped us off and departed for another city back east to minister. No one in America knew where we were. What if something happened to our driver while absent? At the same time my heart was broken over the persecuted church in Poland. These wonderful, educated Believers were desperately poor in worldly commodities. Their Bibles were precious and few. The hymnals they used were worn, handmade, mimeographed copies. But they were joyful. Always abounding, as it were, "in the work of the Lord." In Leszno, they took us to minister in "the church." It was a third floor walk-up apartment crammed with every kind of chair, including plastic ones, plus a vase of colorful flowers. The room quickly filled. People stood wall-to-wall. They reminded me that Leszno had once been the center of the Moravian revival in Poland and home to a great Bible Training Center led by John Amos Comenius. Communist repression could not snuff out the Light that continued to shine in that place.

While kneeling by a log near the pond, I was deeply moved to pray. As the sun peeped over the hill on the eastern shore of the lake, I was audibly worshipping the Lord. I assumed I was alone in my wooded bower. But then I sensed I was being observed. I looked up to see a young man, the village cow catcher, staring at me from rather close up. He was a young red-headed Pole, about seventeen, whose job it was to drive the village cows down to the lake for water—every morning. Then he would head them up and out to pasture. Evenings he reversed the process. He must have heard me praying that morning down by the pond. I wasn't loud. But at this hour the village was quiet, except for the crowing of roosters. I looked up. We caught each other's eyes. I didn't know the Polish word for prayer. So I explained by the sign of praying hands pointed up toward heaven. He grasped the idea. He smiled back at me, a big ear to ear Polish *uśhmiech* (smile).

I have to believe my prayers, along with the saints there at the camp, were effective. Before the week was over, the village commissar and his family and in-laws were all walking with us along the mile-long path to the old mansion and tent. They listened intently to every word of the gospel. And we did get safely back, by way of Prague, Czechoslovakia to the States. Our hearts were thrilled when Mietek, our Polish interpreter, brought news from Warsaw that the Communist government, the church's persecutor, had fallen the very last day of camp. Power would be transferred to freedom-loving Polish dissidents. Christians for years had prayed for this day. The camp sang joyfully, "This is the day the Lord has made. We will rejoice and be glad in it" from Psalm 118:24.

A Spirit-led prayer warrior discerns and obeys the unique leading of the Holy Spirit. The Spirit Himself is the principal intercessor. He prays through the utterances of praying saints. Spiritual prayers go far beyond human perspective and understanding. This requires an exercise of humility and faith, recognizing our weakness and letting the Holy Spirit direct our prayers:

Likewise the Spirit also helps in our weaknesses. For we do not know what we should pray for as we ought, but the spirit Himself makes intercession for us with groanings which cannot be uttered. Now He who searches the hearts knows what the mind of the Spirit is because He makes intercession for the saints according to the will of God.[52]

Any prayer that does not come by way of the Spirit's unction is mere words. Often these words are showy religious performances. Prayer leaders must beware that intense prayer sessions do not slide into religious superstition and repetitious incantations. Sacred seasons of prayer may indeed become specialized and centered on a definite field of action. A group may concentrate its prayer energies, like a laser beam, on one specific target. But effective orations are never woo-woo nor spooky. Beware of the person whose authoritative presence takes charge of the meeting, making an outward show of feigned spirituality. Letting that person take over can lead to chaos and manipulation. Worse still, the end result can be witchcraft and control.

Witchcraft often covers its rebellion against God's set authority with a religious show. It cannot honor nor regard humble, prophetic, prayer-directed leadership. This problem is hardly an issue with women alone. Men can fall into this religious trap as well. The prophet Elijah's ministry hit this head on. Ahab and Jezebel had used their powerful throne to introduce official Baal worship in the land of Israel. Almost all the prophets of the Lord God of Israel were rounded up and summarily executed. In fact, Elijah thought he alone had survived. (Actually 7000 men of God had not bowed their knees to Baal.) In this dastardly cruel deed, Jezebel took the lead. But Ahab was her passive enabler, her accomplice in crime.

Religious witchcraft seeks to control the Holy Spirit led prayer ministry—and thus quell the prophetic voice guiding the church. This spirit of demonic control has wrecked many an effective prayer ministry. It imitates spirituality. But it operates through illegitimate powers. It is no wonder that scripture gives voice to the prophet Samuel's declaration to stubborn Saul: *Behold, to obey is better than sacrifice, and to hearken than the fat of rams. For rebellion is as the sin of witchcraft, and stubbornness is as iniquity and idolatry...* [53]

Prayer Mountain is the highest point overlooking Dallas. At 757 feet it affords a grand view. We learned the hard way that witches prefer to hold sway over cities by occupying the high ground atmosphere. We permit no liberty to that spirit in our prayer meetings. Tozer in his classic book on revival praying *Born After Midnight* warns of this:

"There is but a hairline between truth and superstition. We should learn the truth about the enemy, but we must stand bravely against every superstitious notion he would introduce about himself. The truth will set us free but superstition will enslave us."[54]

Powerful prayer meetings should not be discouraged. The church today is desperate for fervent Spirit led pray-ers. Insipid *Kumbaya* style prayers have left the church toothless in the fight to stave off the war against the family and nation. In times like these, we need to call the church back to real prayer. Our prayer times should last until the breakthrough comes. A.W. Tozer wrote of his conviction that revival in the church is born after midnight—when the saints have gotten down to serious business with God. Thus the reason for the title of his early classic on revival *Born After Midnight*. Jesus said it best, "Men ought always to pray and not give up."[55] We are not quitters nor slackers! Prayer is for those who seek a victorious life in Christ. *Onward Christian soldiers!*

We shall nobly save, or meanly lose the best hope of earth. –Abraham Lincoln, in his Annual Message to Congress, December 1862. A few months later, he would call the Union to a Day of Humiliation, Fasting and Prayer.

"Our fathers believed in sin and the devil and hell as constituting one force; and they believed in God and righteousness and heaven as the other. Man, so our fathers held, had to choose sides; he could not be neutral. For him it must be life or death, heaven or hell, and if he chose to come out on God's side he could expect open war with God's enemies. The fight would be real and deadly and would last as long as life continued here."
–A.W. Tozer,
Playground or Battleground, reprinted from *The City*,
Houston Baptist University, Winter 2009

If the Mountain Could Speak

*Jesus "cleansed" prayer. He found it as magic and
mere petition and left it as communion.
Prayer was no longer getting something out of God,
but God getting something out of us.
It was a pulling of ourselves to God that,
through this high contact with higher power,
higher purpose might be achieved.*
–E. Stanley Jones,
Victorious Living, p. 127; Abingdon-Cokesbury Press, Nashville, TN, 1936

*When the test came, when freedom had to be fought for or abandoned,
they fought. They were soldiers of democracy.*
–Stephen E. Ambrose

CHAPTER EIGHTEEN

HERE IS HOPE!

Oh the hope of Israel, his Savior in times of trouble...
Jeremiah 14:8

*For I know the plans I have for you, declares the Lord, plans to prosper you
and not to harm you, plans to give you hope, and a future. Then you will
call upon Me and come and pray to Me and I will listen to you. You will
seek Me and find Me when you seek me with all your heart.*
Jeremiah 29:11-13 NIV

*Now may the God of hope fill you with all joy and peace in believing,
that you may abound in hope by the power of the Holy Spirit.*
Romans 15:13

*Let us hold fast the confession of our hope without wavering,
for He who promised is faithful.*
Hebrews 10:23

Strength for today and bright hope for tomorrow...
from *Great is Thy Faithfulness*
by Chisholm and Runyan

Little did I know on that hope-filled morning back in '69 when I first glimpsed this mysterious mountain from an airliner's window, that God had destined this promontory as a high place of hope. But He knew. He knew this would be a good place to dispense hope to a big, troubled city. He saw this before the creation of time. I could not have known then that our many experiences, both fun and *unfun*, were training us for such a purpose. There were times when all we had was hope. We banked on the God of hope and held onto His promises for dear life.

"It is good that one should hope," cried the prophet Jeremiah in his most excruciating hour, in his darkest pit, "and wait for the salvation of the Lord."[56] Occasionally the way grew dark for us as well. Time after time we did lots of waiting. Praying. And more waiting. But God who is faithful proves Himself in our adverse challenges. Amazingly His timing was always accurate to the minute. His ways are best. Mysterious, but good all the time.

Some skeptics have quarreled, asking the question why would we even struggle with this rock bound hill to create a set apart place of prayer. Purists have reminded us that God is everywhere and thus needs no certain consecrated place. They are only partly right.

The Lord Over the Mountains, who created sparkling glacier lakes, clear rushing streams tumbling toward oceans, great granite snow-covered peaks, or forests with pure placid ponds reflecting the sun had us humans in mind. He made such places as retreats to preserve mankind's sanity.

Henry David Thoreau wasn't far off the mark when he penned, "In wildness is the preservation of the world." Being out in the wilds among bobcats, bobolinks, raccoons, foxes, and roadrunners refreshes the soul. Big city workers who daily fight traffic and vie for pole position in the rat race of business need to come apart before they come apart. The soul needs an atmosphere of peace. Sometimes a simple walk in the woods refreshes us.

Jesus is the great example. He had a pattern of resorting to wilderness. He often would steal away to the mountains to be alone in prayer with the Father. Sometimes He spent the night under the stars: "Now it came to pass in those days that He went out to the mountain to pray, and continued all night in prayer to God."[57]

We are always amazed at the wide variety of seekers who have come here to find God's hope and peace. Every social class, every color feels welcomed. Those who come broke and down in the dumps mingle with successful leaders with six figure incomes. Most of the recent Dallas mayors of the last twenty years have visited here for prayer. Both our present mayor and our previous mayor met with Southern Dallas pastors here to pray prior to launching their successful election campaigns.

But we are also here for the very desperate—to offer hope. Desperation is not uniquely a poor man's problem. One day back in 1990, I was at work in our temporary mobile office. The hill was still a rough, undeveloped place. Few visitors ventured up our unpaved, rutted road. As I looked out the window, I saw a Jeep coming up, carefully dodging the many large bumps. It was driven by a business suited man.

I stepped out to greet his arrival. I was taken by surprise. It was the mayor of my suburban hometown Duncanville. Mayor Ed Purcell had been my longtime local banker friend. I knew him as a born-again Believer who had received Christ at a Billy Graham crusade in Dallas' Cotton Bowl stadium. He went on to help found a large spiritual Catholic congregation, Holy Spirit Catholic Church, in our city. Everyone in our town seemed to know him. One of his memorable civic projects was the construction of the eternal flame-lit war memorial monument in the city center. Ed was a veritable community fixture, a congenial public institution who knew practically everybody in Duncanville.

Today he appeared worried. Unusually heavy worry lines furrowed his brow. Feeling he was distraught, I took a few minutes just to walk him over the property. At that time there wasn't much to show except the wonderful view of the lake. We sat down at a picnic table to talk.

My friend has never wanted for words. But I felt there was something down deep in his soul that was too painful to articulate. This is the real reason for his visit, I discerned.

"Ed," I suggested, "you've obviously come here for more than talk. What can we pray about? After all, *this is* Prayer Mountain, not *Talk Mountain*."

With that, my friend began to unburden his soul. I listened sympathetically. This man was always a positive minded leader, never a whiner. But he was in pain today. With a practiced dignity he tried to conceal it. But hurt oozed out of his every word.

Due to the current real estate bust, his bank had been struggling. Then he was totally blindsided one day when Federal Deposit Insurance Corporation regulators showed up unannounced. The Feds closed his bank although it was still functioning as a solvent institution. Much of his life had been poured into that firm. He took another position at a smaller bank only to have the board chop his salary in half and fire much of the help. In the midst of this, his marriage shattered. He was devastated by the painful split. Facing financial ruin, he took over his son Patrick's summer job after the high school football season started. That job was hardly prestigious. Patrick had been the evening delivery boy for a local Chinese carry out restaurant. One bright spot: Patrick had a good football season at Duncanville High. But the town's mayor and banker was working evenings delivering food orders. All this just to survive.

Ed was a broken man. Ready to call it quits. Even as he spoke though, he still was straining to keep his chin up. After all, he was Mister Mayor.

I opened my pocket Bible to Jeremiah 29. Before I read the prophet's words, I explained the dire circumstances in which this tough book was written. The prophet Jeremiah walked through the dark night of the soul, weeping all the way. But there is much hope in the powerful word of the Lord he records, especially the promise he receives. It is he who exclaims in his darkest, most discouraging hour:

Through the Lord's mercies we are not consumed
Because His compassions fail not.
They are new every morning;
Great is Your faithfulness![58]

I explained to my friend how that Jeremiah 29 addresses those Jews who have been carried away captive to Babylon. The prophet tells them it is God's will for them to serve out their days there as productive citizens: "This is what the Lord Almighty, the God of Israel says...Seek the peace and the prosperity of the city to which I have carried you...Pray to the Lord for it, because if it prospers, you too will prosper."[59]

We then stopped and prayed for Duncanville and Dallas. I reassured him that our hometown still needed his mayoral leadership. We prayed for wisdom as he led Duncanville's government.

Continuing with Jeremiah's promise, I assured my hurting fellow citizen that this shadowed season of his life would soon pass. As the Lord's Word promises: "I will come to you and fulfill my gracious promise...For I know the plans I have for you, declares the Lord, plans to prosper you and not to harm you, plans to give you hope and a future. Then you will call upon me and come to pray to me, and I will listen to you. You will seek me and find me when you seek me with all your heart. I will be found by you, declares the Lord."[60]

We prayed for hope to return to his soul, as Romans 15:17 promises: "that you may abound in hope by the power of the Holy Spirit." At the final amen, he suddenly remembered he had an appointment to keep. He climbed back into his Jeep and departed down the hill. Returning to his busy life. As I watched him leave, I wondered if I had helped him at all.

I had no way, at the time, of knowing how deep my mayor's despair had been. A day or two later he paused for a friendly conversation with my father. His honesty and refreshing candor startled Dad. "I had planned it out in my mind," Ed told him. He recited the low point of his drive in the hills. "I was actually driving around looking for a place to end it all. I didn't want to go on living. The pain was too much. I'd given up on life.

"Then I saw that mountain. I remembered. You all pray up there. I felt I was being pulled to turn in and drive up that steep, rough road. I hardly expected to find anyone there. Your son Robert happened to be there. So we talked and prayed a few minutes. God's healed my broken heart. His Spirit has restored my confidence. I'm on top of things now. God is good."

Dad called me with Ed's surprising assessment of that seeming insignificant twenty minute visit. The Lord did put Mr. Ed back on top. He continued to serve as mayor of Duncanville's diverse population of over 40,000 citizens. Banking was his business. He soon headed another successful bank in town. Eventually he remarried and lived to tell his story of the Holy Spirit's leading him back to hope in Christ. He has never quite retired. He is too busy enjoying life to be depressed. He found God's promise to be true that day on the mountain. No night is so dark that we cannot see Him.

Mountain Creek Church today has a well-trained suicide prevention team. It is led by a retired U.S. Army Chaplain who specialized in training others in how to deal with post traumatic syndrome. This includes suicidal and depression cases. Hope is available to all who seek it. We are blessed with many amazing stories of God turning despair into hope. Too many to tell here.

Not all cases come to us. Sometimes we get their emergency calls late at night. Such was the desperate call from a household in crisis. A despondent family member with a hangman's noose around his neck was threatening to kick the chair out from under his trembling body. In plain sight of the whole family! Our team rushed over and spent hours saving this one. It was worth it. The family is now one of the most beautiful, helpful families in our congregation.

We offer hope on this mountain. The gospel of Jesus Christ is all about hope. God's news is good news. His will for us is good, filled with hope, joy and peace in the Holy Spirit.

Redemptive hope is our simple message. Not religion, which is all about human achievement—man striving to get to God. Life in the Spirit is understanding that God has come to us in the form of Jesus, the Son of God. He is the Word become flesh: *Ave verum corpus!*

Because of the work of the Holy Spirit, our story has no ending. We can identify with the Book of Acts, a book which has no formal ending, no closing section, no final word of benediction. The work goes on.

The testimony of faith is that, no matter how things look in this fallen world, all God's acts are wrought in perfect wisdom.
–A.W. Tozer in *The Knowledge of the Holy,* Harper's San Francisco, p. 62

CHAPTER NINETEEN

REFLECTIONS ON MOVING A MOUNTAIN

The effective, fervent prayer of a righteous man avails much.
James 5:16

Great is Thy faithfulness! Morning by morning new mercies I see.
From the hymn "Great is Thy Faithfulness"

*Being confident of this that he who began a good work in you will carry it
on to completion until the day of Jesus Christ.*
Philippians 1:6

*Small deeds done are better than great deeds planned.
We cannot do everything. But help us to do something.
For Jesus' sake, Amen.*
–U.S. Senate Chaplain Peter Marshall in his short prayer written for the opening
session of the Senate. He died suddenly two days before the opening. His prayer
was read posthumously.

The Lord has used quite a remarkable team over the years to build up Prayer Mountain. We have enjoyed an amazing assortment of characters, most of which were your garden variety Christians. We have had fiddlers, mechanics, engineers, government workers, nuclear plant operators, heavy equipment operators, born-again lawyers, veterinarians, medical doctors, dentists, linguists, automobile dealers, retired pastors, ex-spies, and military officers. They come to us from all backgrounds and denominations, including a few heathen. They represent diverse language families and skin colors. Caucasians, Hispanics, African-Americans, Africans, American Indians, Caribbean Islanders, Czechs, Romanians, Koreans, and Pakistanis. You name it. And this is but a short list of the whole mix. They have all played a part in the work of the ministry here. This disparate group of servant-hearted folk labored together in creating this place. It was an arduous task. But together it was fun.

Back in the fall of 2005, we were about halfway finished on the construction of our Summit fellowship hall. We were on a cash pay-as-we-build basis. Then we finally ran out of cash when the structure was barely in the dry. It was an enclosed shell of a building. Some of our elders felt stymied and advised us to lock it up and ring it with yellow "keep out" tape. It seemed none of our mountains would move when we spoke to them. I dug in and insisted we keep at least two men working: Lindell Buck, a retired pastor and experienced church builder and J.D. Dowd, our heavy equipment operator.

We prayed, and the elders gave us grace to continue by faith, one week at a time. We sought for a divine solution. In our congregational gatherings we teach the Biblical blessing of giving, but never push nor badger the congregation to give money. We believe that we construct buildings with offerings. Tithes are given to run the living ministry of the church. Spirit led giving works best without pressure and manipulation.

Yet here we were, out of operating cash except for weekly budget needs. We still had one remaining alternative. We had land, plenty of it. We could survey and plat some more city lots for sale over on the far east side of our property. This land fronted a city street in a lovely residential neighborhood. Only one problem. One very big problem! That street front property was buried under a giant mound of excavation spoil. The previous developer, Centennial Homes Corporation, in 1985 had bulldozed down a sizable knoll which stood in the center of their initial phase one property development. They just moved it with giant excavators and dumped it on what eventually would become the property we purchased in 1998. It was mostly huge boulders and chalky limestone material. All of this eventually settled over the years. Regrowth of cedars, oaks, and cottonwoods adorned the small manmade mountain. It was at least 20 feet high, 40 feet wide, and nearly 400 feet long. It looked like a giant misplaced earthen dam. If ever we hoped to plat that street frontage land into city lots, we would have to excavate and move out that big berm.

J.D. Dowd was game to try. We began with a John Deere 550 crawler with a big dozer blade. After five days we had barely scraped the top off that mountain of spoil. We were in an unseasonably warm, dry winter. Dust was blowing everywhere. Fortunately the stiff southern breeze was blowing the dust away from the neighborhood. The stout little excavator was not the best machine for the job. We rented a larger machine. A week later we still had a least 60 per cent of that mound left to move. We brought in a D7 Caterpillar. Things began to move, finally. J.D. loved it.

Now I faced another problem. J.D. had been experiencing some heart problems. He had arrhythmic symptoms. There was a possibility of his fainting out cold. He insisted he was doing fine. I wasn't so sure.

I walked out of our offices one day. I could hear that big dozer 300 yards away in the woods, moving material. Suddenly an awful, disturbing fear hit me. What if J.D. fainted while at the controls! He could wreck the neighborhood across from our property! That big diesel Cat was big enough to smash its way through houses. I grabbed some bottled water and hastened through the woods to J.D. and his loud, menacing track machine, fretting as I went. I was greatly relieved to find J.D. in good spirits. But he was absolutely covered in a fine dust. He was barely recognizable. The dust was blowing in small dust devils and was now all over me. J.D. was finally half way through the grinding mountain moving ordeal. None of us had figured it would be this tough a task. We had to transform that firm, backbreaking hill into a gentle slope toward the city street. Otherwise our lots could not be platted with Dallas. We were all dirty and really tired of what we had naively thought might be just a three or four day excavation project. It was beginning to be an exasperating four week Dust Bowl of Discouragement. We were locked in a big fight between us and that hard rock, unmoving mountain. It was a dirty fight.

I walked away troubled and emotionally drained. While dusting off my clothes, I cried out to the Lord. "Oh God," I complained, "does it always have to be so tough? Can't You make it easy? Please, God. I'm tired of it always being so hard. Do something, if You will. Can You make it easier?"

The Lord immediately responded to my spirit. *I can certainly make it easy,* He replied, *but that will not make it better.* It was one of the clearest, quickest answers I have ever received. I was STUNNED! In speaking to me, the Lord suddenly opened my spiritual eyes to see all the faithful, mighty men He had brought us. It was like a quick, flashing slideshow of photos of these good men. They were hale and hardy adventurers, stout-hearted and passionate about enduring. What a blessing they were. All of them, fearless in the face of hardships. Not quitters. The quitters had left us long before. The slackers fled. The hard struggle scared them all away. Certainly a few men left for valid reasons. But a remnant had remained faithful and true. Then other good men, seeking a group of real, faithful, red-blooded males joined up with our remnant. Suddenly I could see an obvious pattern. Those real men loved a challenge! Such men are, in the words of author John Eldridge, a band of brothers and *Wild at Heart*. Hey, that's our guys! It is a fact that we now typically have more guys than ladies. More brothers than sisters. Men have loved this mountain and its vigorous challenges. Even the 40 voice choir, which JoAn conducts, often has more singing men than women.

If I'd had it my way, I certainly would have made it all easier and much more entertaining. In my walk back through the woods of Prayer Mountain over to our offices, I could not help but repent for my foolish fretting. God did it His way. And it was best. I should have known. Not always fun and games, but best. God's wisdom is so beyond the grasp of my poor mind.

We finally did get those lots platted and sold. The Summit building was eventually finished and beautifully furnished. Its interior décor reflects the strong men who made it possible. It does not look like so many traditional church facilities. Instead of the typical grandmother's living room appearance, it looks like an outback mountain lodge where great hunters meet and tell glowing stories of high adventure. Real men stories.

I could never have figured out such an unconventional plan. Only the Holy Spirit could have dreamed up this concept. What better way to attract real men than to involve them in the rugged challenge of a mountain. We can all try to conquer a small mountain! We are blessed by these brothers, husbands, dads, and granddads. They are a company of iron men. Good to the bone. Compassionate. Caring. Giving. Serving. Men who overcame giants by the power of prayer and the Word.

Out of the struggles has come a deep sense of our mission of compassion. We are blessed to share our bread with many. When suffering Job defends his character to his detractors, he attests to his unselfish generosity: "If I have kept the poor from their desire," he protests, "or eaten my morsel by myself so the fatherless could not eat of it..."[61] He simply informs the voluntary panel of critics and comforters hearing his case that he did not eat "by myself." Enough said. This one characteristic, unselfishness, is why many missionaries live among desperately needy Third World people. They refuse to eat their bread alone, by themselves. We can take comfort in the fact that God has many compassionate, caring people everywhere following in the footsteps of Jesus. That is amazing grace!

In the midst of a self-absorbed, self-centered "It's all about me" generation of rock stars, movie stars, and other greedy public figures, this is refreshing news. In fact, I am convinced that how you handle the unseen, unsung mercy task is one of the true marks of godliness. The Good Samaritan is an enduring example of this truth. The man in Jesus' story forever transformed the racial term *Samaritan* from a slur to a badge of honor. By his good deed alone. Now thousands of compassion ministries the world over proudly call themselves by that name which was once a term of cold-hearted loathing. We thank God for Good Samaritans everywhere. What would we do without them?

*Far better it is to dare mighty things, to win glorious triumphs
even though checkered by failures, than to rank with those poor spirits
who neither enjoy much nor suffer much because they live in the gray
twilight that knows not victory or defeat.*
–Theodore Roosevelt

Every man dies, but not every man lives.
–William Wallace

*Success is to be measured not so much by the position that
one has reached in life as by the obstacle which he has overcome.*
–Booker T. Washington

*Children of the heavenly Father
Safely in his bosom gather;
Nestling bird or star in heaven
Such a refuge ne'er was given.*
From *Children of the Heavenly Father* by Caroline Berg,
set to an old Swedish folk tune

CHAPTER TWENTY

STONE OF HELP

Then Samuel took a stone and set it up...and called its name Ebenezer
(stone of help) saying, "Thus far the Lord has helped us."
1 Samuel 7:12

The building block that was rejected became the cornerstone of a whole new world.
From the song, *Building Block* by Noel Paul Stookey
of Peter, Paul, and Mary fame.

In the autumn of 2006 we were completing the Summit building. J.D. Dowd was operating the big backhoe tractor "dressing up the construction site" as he called it. He was pushing aside some rather large boulders, moving them away from the facility. Most of the stones were too large to lift in the front loader bucket. So J.D. was shoving them with the big diesel machine. As he pushed one huge stone over on the northwest side of the new building, he was surprised to see the stone flip up on its side and stand upright. J.D. left it momentarily to move more rocks. After a few more maneuvers, he returned, intending to push the big rock over flat on the ground, lest it pose a safety hazard. As he approached, J.D. was struck by the appearance of the upright stone as it was outlined against the blue sky. He thought it bore a striking resemblance to our Mountain Creek logo, used in all our stationery.

J.D. was excited when he appeared at my study door. "Pastor, you've got to come see this," he insisted.

"See what?" I puzzled.

"Pastor, I cain't tell you. I gotta show you. Ya got a minute?"

I followed J.D. over to the front yard of the Summit. "There!" he pointed, jabbing his finger for emphasis.

"What? Are you pointing to that great big rock?" I quizzed.

J.D. nodded.

Suddenly I saw it. Recognizing the shape of our mountain logo, I exclaimed, "J.D., where'd you find that?"

"It was just in that collection of boulders I was going to buttress up the high end of the backfill with," he answered. "It didn't fit there, so I shoved it out of the way." He grinned his big, engaging grin.

We stood there marveling at the coincidental match; the stone's likeness to our familiar design logo of a mountain. Seeing it stand there, I was concerned it might be a safety hazard. I ventured over to give it a hefty shove. Nothing budged. The rock wasn't even shaky. It stood there steadfast and unmoved.

We both agreed it needed to be there. To me it was like *Ebenezer*, the prophet Samuel's monumental *Stone of Help*. The prophet had raised up this stone to commemorate God's answering his prayer for help in turning back the Philistine attack on Israel at Mizpah.[62] Samuel christened the stone *Ebenezer*, declaring, "Thus far has the Lord helped us."

J.D. offered to permanently encase the stone's base with concrete and steel. He had it all done before lunchtime. Thus on that late autumn morning in 2006, in the words of the old classic hymn, we did "raise our Ebenezer"[63] to the Lord.

We could never have guessed what would happen next. A week later a young, skinny, former Abilene Christian University student named Rusty showed up at the mountain. He was hungry, out of work, down and out, and too proud to ask for help. On closer questioning it seemed his life was all bound up in knots of failure. He was homeless. Homeless at Thanksgiving and Christmas time! Could we help him find some kind of holiday job so he could take Christmas money to his estranged wife and family?

We temporarily housed him in our security cabin. "What kind of work can you do?" we asked. Turns out he was a starving artist, really the genuine article. He was an unemployed stone carver—with little money or fame. He had labored alongside his mentor who was a famous crafter and creator of titanic mountainside carvings. But alas, the teacher went broke trying to produce a colossal likeness of Mount Rushmore in rural West Texas, located on a 300 foot limestone bluff between Abilene and Buffalo Gap, Texas. It was to feature Sam Houston, Davy Crockett, William B. Travis, and Stephen Austin. The enigmatic but talented stone carver's huge project shut down for lack of money.

To prove his story was not a fabrication, Rusty offered to go back to West Texas, fetch his tools, and then come carve a message on our big rock. We approved his plan. J.D. drove him out to Abilene and back. We put him to work on the Ebenezer stone the next day.

Our choice of text for the rock was a handwritten statement from Dad Summers' 1942 edition Bible flyleaf. (He had passed away in 2004.) It had been a favorite expression of his.

CHRIST FOR US—the foothills

CHRIST IN US—the Summit

Across the bottom of the monument stone we applied the verse from 1 Samuel 7:12, "Hitherto hath the Lord helped us." I wanted it written in stone: in hard rock. For truly God has helped us.

That Christmas we inaugurated the Summit with a grand Christmas party complete with choirs, carols, Joseph, Mary, a baby in the manger, shepherds and wise men. J.D.'s big rock now named Ebenezer was a monument to the occasion. Who knew? Who knew we would have an indigent rock carver come chisel scriptures on a great stone that had amazingly stood up when it was being shoved out of the way? Only the Lord could have known. Every spring Ol' Ebenezer rock is surrounded by Texas bluebonnets. A wonderful memorial to the help of the Lord.

We sent the artist back home with his pockets loaded. To his enduring wife we gifted a fine old Chrysler Fifth Avenue auto. Last we heard, our stone carver soon disappeared into the world of destitute itinerant artists. A rolling stone.

With the Summit now complete, we turned our attention to remodeling the older Fireside Room fellowship hall into our 24 hour/always open prayer center. Beginning in 2003, Lindell Buck, a retired church builder and pastor on our staff, began praying in the sanctuary at 7:14 am every morning in reference to Solomon's great prayer in 2 Chronicles 7:14. J.D. and other men began to join with him. Our facilities had been opened up by J.D. every morning at 6:00 am for early prayers. John Price, Jr. a young, local pastor and the son of a well-known Dallas County commissioner, made it a habit to come early to pray. Eventually small groups of intercessors from a dozen or so different congregations regularly appeared for seasons of early prayer. So it was time to furnish a place exclusively dedicated to these praying God-seekers.

Our former fellowship hall was perfect. It had a massive fireplace and small kitchen for serving coffee, tea, and hot chocolate. Paul and Britainie Nelson, our prayer pastors who had been leaders in the prayer movement at Dallas Baptist University, took on the renovation project. They brought in fresh paint, new flooring, and design appointments. Finally, we needed prayer teams. They began to train interns. Their efforts are now paying off. The beautiful large room is open and frequented by worshipers and praying people from many congregations.

Building an effective Prayer Center is somewhat like constructing a beautiful European cathedral. It takes time. It's not going to happen overnight. Because JoAn and I are interested in history and architecture, we have enjoyed visiting the great centers of the ancient Christian faith. The list of historic church structures we've visited is long. It's hard to choose a favorite. Perhaps the top three would include Canterbury Cathedral in England, Notre Dame in Paris, and the great marble Cathedral of Milan, Italy. They are marvels of ancient architecture and engineering.

Building a cathedral is a multigenerational project. So also is the development of an effective prayer center. In cathedral construction, someone had to have a plan and a vision. Others had to take up the cause to finish it. No one could get in a hurry. Completion was always out there in the future. Another younger generation would take responsibility and the work continued. On Prayer Mountain we will never get to the place where we can say, "There. We are done. We now have a Prayer Center." Every season of planning and building has been fun and fruitful.

I am amazed at how God's work always gets done. I've wished for—but had little help from—millionaires and professionals with encyclopedic credentials. Maybe that will someday come. Common folks and students have built this mountaintop work. They put forth the effort. God gave the increase.

We've had a few things happen, however, where we did not have to lift a hand or even break a sweat. For instance, the sixteen miles of professional mountain bike trails stretching over our hills and down our canyons are an absolute engineering feat. They are a thrilling gift. Dallas Off-road Bicycle Association (DORBA) has cheerfully supplied the expertise and materials to build the premiere bike trails in Texas, the Big Cedar Wilderness Trails. We supplied the forested ridges; they furnished the creative design and manpower. These popular, picturesque trails, designed by Paul Shadow Johns, are the site of frequent state rallies and races involving a multitude of bikers from all over the country. Some of their hairpin trails down through the canyons should have a warning sign, *Prepare to meet thy God,* at the trailhead.

Actually there is something very scriptural about all this. In Isaiah 58, the famous prayer and fasting chapter of the Bible, we read the promise that if "…you shall delight yourself in the Lord; I will cause you to ride the high hills of the earth."[64] Isaiah's word sure sounds good to me. It seems he foresees us riding mountain bikes on the Big Cedar Wilderness trails here on the mountain. And yes, JoAn and I ride at times. We are more comfortable riding the gentle backwoods trails, along with our loping dogs.

JoAn and I grew up on the Gulf Coast. We remember running from hurricanes. The big storm, Hurricane Carla, devastated the upper Texas Coast, as well as parts of my community. But Carla also helped me through my first year of college: there was so much repair and rebuilding work available for every able bodied person. I had plenty of part time jobs.

Meteorologists know that such massive hurricanes have tiny origins. They all can be traced back to some infinitesimal, almost immeasurable beginning. Weathermen call this the *Butterfly Effect*. Given the supporting atmospheric conditions, some micro breeze as small as a butterfly flitting along the West Coast of Africa can create the seed of disturbed air that may eventually grow into a Category 5, world changing storm.

Praying people who walk in the Spirit of Christ are the moral equivalent of the *Butterfly Effect*. Prayer seems so small and insignificant. Up against big opposition and bad odds, it seems the chance of prayer to trump the powers of evil appears laughable. But the prophet reminds us to be careful with such pessimism: *who can despise the day of small things?*[65] Every great movement has small beginnings. The Judeo Christian religion, on which the social codes of Western civilization are founded, began with the westward call of an itinerant shepherd. This solitary figure, Abraham, was known by the altars he built and his profound belief in God and His promises. The Christian faith began with Jesus and twelve disciples.

I am reminded of an incident which highlighted our own small beginnings. It happened with a group of praying college students in my regular Monday night discipleship gathering. This company of committed college youth came pouring into Praise Chapel one evening. They took their places in the tiered seating rows of the chapel. They were positioned in a way where they could look down to where I stood talking and writing on the drawing board. These were bright young students. Many were involved as campus leaders in sports and student affairs. Most were from Dallas Baptist University, which is just up the parkway from our hilltop. All had been involved in a campus prayer revival. They were fervent.

That particular evening I was teaching some very simple and basic techniques on reading the Word of God. I glanced up on the top row of the chapel seats. A young man was peering out the western windows—and obviously doing so intently. I turned to look for myself. There was a breathtakingly brilliant red orange sunset reflected over the lake.

I stopped my dialogue and invited the whole class to look out the western windows. Some of the observers exclaimed at the wonder and beauty of this late winter sunset. The whole western scene was gilded with a rosy glow.

It was in that moment that I remembered the encouraging word I had received from my friend Cleddie Keith years ago. Twenty-two years to be sure. He wanted to go find that mountain top wherein he had seen in a visionary experience where I would be teaching young people. This all began with a word. Something too small to hold in the grasp of your hand: the spoken *rhema* word of the Lord.

I mentioned this small beginning to the group of students. One of the senior students, Chase, spoke up. He was the most fervent in spirit. "My life changed with a word at a small prayer gathering," he exclaimed. "A simple word of God's love from my dorm mate, Jared." Chase was a living miracle. In his own words, he had a triple addiction: drugs, alcohol, and fornication. His life had been an absolute mess, which manifested physically in epileptic seizures. Chase was different now, having been made whole by the power of Christ. Through the prayerful witness of his dorm buddy—which he at first adjudged *weird*—he now was set free. Today he is a young executive and a very good evangelist.

In the remaining portion of our gathering, the class talked about how the tipping point of life can change with a simple word or incident. A word can change our thinking. Most of the original class of students moved on with their careers. Others stayed here with us. They assisted us in *Fire on the Mountain,* our college ministry's contemporary worship services, led by Carey Rholdon. Some emerged as leaders in our local work. DBU graduates Paul and Britainie Nelson were married here on the mountain. They served first as Youth Pastors. Later they helped us found the World Prayer Center. This ministry has become one of the strongest components of the work on the mountain. Prayer constantly goes on in that attractive Prayer Center with its big stone fireplace: continuous worship and prayer night and day. Rarely would you find this mountain without praying groups of people.

The stories of the beloved Bible heroes make for an entertaining read today. But we must remember that in reality they were real nail-biters, filled with throbbing angst. Prayer made the difference in the outcome. Who and what you become is determined by how and what you pray. Long before the little shepherd lad David met big Goliath on the battlefield, he had a well-developed prayer life. When David's moment of destiny came, he was well prepared for it even though the Word says "there was no sword in the hand of David."[66] He was just a kid with a slingshot who knew "the battle is the Lord's."[67]

There are times in which we all feel inadequate and not very well armed, but the battle is not ours. It is the Lord's. When my son was eight years old, he drew a picture of his Sunday School lesson. It was a pen and ink rendering of little David standing over the huge fallen dead body of Goliath. His caption read: *It's great to be big. It's bigger to be great.*

"Big" in Dallas is *everything!* In our town everything's got to be big in order to project an air of importance, maybe even omnipotence. But size never determines effectiveness. The Lord was able to create something effective here. It had little to do with big crowds, big talk, or big bucks.

If we could somehow measure the Spirit of the Living God, we would discover He fills all time and all space: *all in all.* His love has no limits. His power has no measure. His wisdom knows no boundary. His love never fails. Great is His faithfulness. Who can measure Him?

You are the light of the world—like a city on a hilltop that cannot be hidden.
Matthew 5:14 NLT

Don't just pretend to love others. Really love them. Hate what is wrong. Hold tightly to what is good. Love each other with genuine affection and take delight in honoring each other. Never be lazy, but work hard and serve the Lord enthusiastically. Rejoice in our confident hope. Be patient in trouble, and keep on praying. When God's people are in need, be ready to help them. Always be eager to practice hospitality. Bless those who persecute you. Don't curse them; pray that god will bless them.
Romans 12:9-14 NLT

*We have the privilege not only of plumbing the depths
of the knowledge of God, but also of scaling the heights.*
–Des Evans

CHAPTER TWENTY-ONE

THE GENERATION THAT SEEKS HIS FACE

Yet who knows whether you have come to the kingdom
for such a time as this?
Esther 4:14

Who may ascend into the hill of the Lord?
Or who may stand in His holy place?
He who has clean hands and a pure heart,
who has not lifted up his soul to an idol,
nor sworn deceitfully... This is Jacob,
the generation of those who seek Him,
who seek Your face.
Psalm 24:3,4,6

O Lord, You have made us for Thyself,
and our hearts are restless until they find their rests in Thee.
–Augustine

In the last days, God says, I will pour out My Spirit on all people.
Your sons and daughters will prophesy.
Your young men will see visions,
your old men dream dreams.
Acts 2:17

A tidal wave, a virtual tsunami is sweeping toward us. Get ready, NOW!

A youthful generation of God-seekers is emerging. They long for the supernatural presence of the Lord. They are willing to linger in prayer and search out the depths of the Spirit of the Lord. It is decision time for America, and they know it. They also know that only a great spiritual awakening can save this nation.

Here on the mountain we know that all our labors have served to prepare us for this moment in time. This is our destiny. But it is not for us alone. It is a moment of truth for the whole Church. We need to know this is our moment of truth, our own rendezvous with destiny. A whole generation has dropped out of the Church. But a younger generation is coming back. It is a reentry time. It's homecoming day in the Church.

There is a critical, possibly fatal moment whenever a space capsule rockets back into the earth's atmosphere. A very brief window of opportunity opens. There is a precise moment and angle of reentry in order for the capsule to slip back through. Too steep and the capsule burns up in the earth's atmosphere. Too shallow in its angle of banking and it skips off into space. Lost forever in space. We dare not miss the opportunity.

The Church today must have the prayer inspired guidance of the Holy Spirit. We have an experienced Pilot at the controls. Prayer keeps us in close contact with Mission Control.

My moment of truth came as a surprise when I was a high school student. In the winter of 1960, a once-in-a-century snowstorm, a freak event, clobbered Houston. The city practically shut down for three days. Schools were closed. The rare snow days were my brief window of opportunity. No classes. No ball practice. No running the roads. No nothing. But my home church did not cancel its services.

Leonard Ravenhill, the well-known author on prayer and revival, had come to our home church. This man of God from Yorkshire, England (who had just moved to the States) was the most passionate God-seeking man I had ever encountered. A fellow disciple, Ernie Trotter, was driving him around the country in Trotter's impressive new Volvo sports sedan. I became the backup chauffeur for these two when Trotter's Volvo was left at the dealer's service center awaiting some missing part.

In Ravenhill's Yorkshire English, I was to come *collect* the two of them and drive to the meeting. This arrangement put me in close proximity to the man of God. From time to time he recounted interesting incidents from his past travels. I was fascinated. There were times I arrived to *collect* the ministers, times when they would be so deep in prayer that I had trouble summoning them to the door. An uneasy sense of conviction swept over me. I felt undone. My faith, and the lack thereof, was challenged. Night after night Ravenhill concluded his strong, anointed messages with a call to prayer. I went forward, as did many of my high school pals. We lingered. The presence of God was awesome. The result was that we students recommitted our lives to the Lord's leadership.

Afterwards we painted and refurbished an unused room in the church facility. We made it comfortable. It was our prayer room. That was my first *prayer center*. It was a small beginning but we put it to good use. From time to time we conducted all night prayer vigils there, strong enthusiastic prayer meetings.

Everything changed in our group with that season of spiritual awakening. Even the sporting atmosphere of our hunting and fishing campouts was transformed. We went on to form a pretty good Southern gospel quartet. Our senior year of high school was filled with weekend travels around the state, conducting youth meetings. Most of the singers in our quartet went on through College on scholarships and would become pastors, counselors, and Christian college professors.

After college at Sam Houston State University, JoAn and I taught high school in Houston's North Shore communities. A highlight of that season was when I was faculty advisor for Houston's largest Youth for Christ club at North Shore High. All this was equipping JoAn and me to serve as shepherds and teachers in the coming *Jesus Movement* which swept America in the late 1960's and early 1970's. Another highlight of this period was working closely with the young Jewish disciple, Bob Weiner, who had an anointing to reach college campuses with the gospel. Many dynamic young leaders emerged from his intense training program known as Maranatha Leadership Training Schools. Bob connected better with talented cutting-edge students than with former hippies. He trained many of today's Christian community leaders.

The *Jesus Movement* was big on worship. It established a new pattern of spiritual praise and worship teams which fill the platforms in today's fast growing contemporary Christian congregations. But more importantly, the movement spared America from the spirit of revolution and anarchy that seriously threatened university campuses in the late 1960's. Many campus radicals, even high profile ones, found peace with God during the *Jesus Movement* era. They soon became influential teachers. Art Katz, a Marxist Jew from Berkeley, California, was destined to become one such spokesman and an early leader in the nascent Messianic Jewish expression. But he was first known by the police at Berkeley for manning the makeshift barricades, put up by the war protestors on campus. Disenchanted with the futility of his life, Art set out to hitch rides through Europe so he could personally engage with European thinkers and philosophers. On a rain-soaked highway in Switzerland, a kindly Believer offered him a ride. He also fed him and gave him a New Testament. This encounter inspired Art to go on to Israel where he hoped to meet with disciples of the late Martin Buber, the famous Jewish philosopher. In Jerusalem, the searching young Marxist was divinely led to a Christian bookstore, where he found hospitality and board. There he also found the Lord *Yeshua* (Hebrew for *Jesus*). His life was radically changed.

Art became a brilliant defender of the gospel. Speaking with erudite candor on many college campuses, Art's demeanor was always intense and passionate. There is no telling how many lives he touched in his lectures and campus encounters. He was powerful.

Today all the leading indicators point to the fact that we are at the cusp of something much bigger than previous awakenings. Prayer always precedes revival. It sparks the fire of revival. We are witnessing a surge, a sweeping prayer revival in young America. All over the nation, in many cities and towns, houses of prayer—prayer centers—are being opened. Fervent, effectual prayers are going up to heaven for a national youth revival in these emerging places. These small-scale operations may not impress the skeptics. But God certainly gives grace to the humble, while resisting the proud. However, these houses of prayer are not isolated, experimental works. Most are networked with older established, high profile congregations. And their leaders are tutored by respected congregational leaders. Thus they are all the more effective in their communities.

This widespread rise of such well-ordered prayer ministries is a harbinger of a coming spiritual awakening. All Bible prophecy suggests a last great Holy Spirit outpouring will precede the Second Coming of Jesus Christ. The Apostle Peter preached such a message on the Day of Pentecost, borrowing the prophecy of Joel: "And it shall come to pass in the last days, says God, that I will pour out of my Spirit on all flesh; your sons and your daughters shall prophesy. Your young men shall see visions, your old men dream dreams. And on My servants and on My handmaidens, I will pour out My Spirit and they shall prophesy."[68] I believe the Jesus Movement, now four decades past, was only a forerunner to the above described last days revival. The big move of God is coming.

People love to come up to the mountain and pray at night. Sitting on one of the westward facing prayer decks, they can peer across a moonlit lake and beyond to a vast sea of glowing city lights. The lighted skyline of downtown Fort Worth occupies the distant horizon some twenty-five miles west. When we began twenty-six years ago, most of this region was dark, open land. Sprawling urban growth has filled in many of the blank spots with malls, schools, expressways, and industrial parks. We got here just in time. Never has our city stood more in the need of prayer. Finally the Church is coming together, united in prayer. We did not invent prayer and we are hardly the only people praying.

Over 50 million unborn humans have had their lives snuffed out since our courts in Roe v. Wade struck down laws protecting the innocent unborn. It all started here in Dallas. Although Dallas District Attorney, Henry Wade won the case for the unborn, the 5th Circuit Court in Louisiana ruled against him. My African-American pastor friend at Fair Park Bible Fellowship, Stephen Brodin, publicly decries the fact that of the 50 plus million abortions since Roe v. Wade, the overwhelming majority are African-Americans. This causes him to weep. He laments the tragic reality that a whole generation of Martin Luther King Jrs., George Washington Carvers, Booker T. Washingtons, Rosa Parks, athletes, singers, pastors, principals, school teachers, scientists, soldiers, wage earners, tax paying citizens and consumers have been lost forever. Nothing less than a great movement of prayer is the last best hope we have on the earth to change this culture of death which pervades our nation. Pastor Brodin sees this genocide against his people as driven by both demonic and political forces.

Change is coming. We have a new dedicated generation of young people "the generation of those who seek Him, who seek Your face!"[69] They understand that praying believers are the most powerful people in the city. They never use the common church excuse: "It is *only* a prayer meeting." They understand the spiritual impact of prayer. It is important. Only prayer can change our nation.

Intercessors from this younger, praying generation handle well the gifts of the Holy Spirit, especially the gifts of healing. At the same time they easily grasp the divine order in which these spiritual gifts operate. For one, they seek a generational impartation. They desire to receive what older, more experienced leaders have to impart. They are open, but very *Berean*-like, in that they search the scriptures for authentication of doctrine.

We have been a witness to some remarkable miracles of healing on this mountain—through prayer. A few healings have been aided by some very good, godly doctors. Others were instant and miraculous.

An interesting healing is the remarkable story of Larry Anderson, who is now a part of our praise team. Larry and Rachel married in 2001. A beautiful daughter was born to them in 2008. Three months later Larry discovered a lump under his right arm. His doctor suggested a biopsy. The test proved to be metastatic melanoma, a rare form of cancer. Larry then went to M.D. Anderson clinic in Houston where doctors removed 40 of his lymph nodes.

In Larry's own words, here is what happened next:

A friend of mine at Mountain Creek suggested we attend a service that was held on a Monday night. I gladly agreed to attend. It wasn't a normal service. It was more of a worship service, with a visiting worship band. A lot of praise and prayer.

Some of the congregation knew of my situation and immediately reached out to us and prayed for us. My wife and I immediately felt the love and presence of the Lord. That night Jim Mackey laid hands on me and prayed a powerful prayer of healing over me. I was like, slain in the Spirit that very night. My wife and I both grew up Catholic, and while she had visited some charismatic churches growing up, I had not. Personally I was not really aware of the meaning of having hands laid on me. Nor certainly did I know the meaning of this being "slain in the Spirit." I could not doubt the power of God. It was so strong. I must have lain on my back on the carpet for ten minutes. (Editor's note: Jim Mackey was also stunned.)

That evening at Mountain Creek had such a powerful impact on our lives. In March 2009, my wife and I both rededicated our lives to the Lord and we were baptized there in the church for the first time in our lives.

After six months my scans showed three new tumors in my liver! It was not looking good for me. I had gone from stage three to a stage four diagnosis. I asked my doctor honestly what was my prognosis now with the cancer in my liver. He replied that he'd give me less than a year to live. This was devastating and crippling news to hear. It was then that the Lord came into our hearts with the assurance He would never leave us. Our prayers moved to a whole new level. We knew He was with us—and He was mostly carrying us.

I began chemo treatments. This proved to be the roughest of the treatments. I lost a lot of weight. And hair. My body looked as if it had been burned from head to toe. All this proved to be unsuccessful in arresting the tumors. I underwent a total of five different treatments.

On the weekends I was home, we were in services having our brothers and sisters pray for us. The elders would anoint my head with oil and pray God's healing prayers over me, while rebuking this disease. Through all their prayers, I learned to pray for myself. I had several church members point out healing scripture promises to claim over my life:

By His stripes I am healed. 1 Peter 2:24 and Isaiah 53:5

For with God nothing will be impossible. Luke 1:37

I am the Lord that heals you. Exodus 15:26

He sent His word and healed them. Psalm 107:20

In the meantime, my wife Rachel began sending out updated emails to keep our church family and all our friends and family current on my progress. Our friends and family then would forward her emails to their friends and families. People in many other churches, whom we have never met, heard about us and sent cards telling us they were praying for us! We were blown away. Absolutely blessed and thankful. I remember standing in our kitchen with my wife feeling overwhelmed by the grace of God. We knew too that we wanted to be part of a congregation that believed in claiming God's powerful Word through continuous prayer.

Throughout this whole process, the church at Mountain Creek stood behind us in full force. We would have people praying with us and for us before service, during service, and after service. And even when we weren't there, we heard of prayers at staff meetings, choir practice, and in the home church gatherings. Again and again the Spirit of the Lord was just pouring over us His great love and peace. I remember Pastor Robert Summers speaking about divine healing and saying that healing can also be a process. He would encourage me with, "Larry, you can't have a testimony without a test." I am here today and stand as a witness to these very same words.

Today I have gained back all the weight I had lost to chemo treatments. I feel good. I am strong in mind, in body, and especially in faith. The tumors on my liver have been greatly reduced and are only a shadow on my tests. I stand here together with my family, my church, and my God. I am years beyond the

217

one year my doctor gave me to live. I give all the praise and glory to my Lord and Savior Jesus Christ.

Only the gospel and power of Christ can change hearts. America cannot be morally renovated merely by the *fiat* of law. We need a revival in every praying church in the land. A generation must be willing to pray until Holy Spirit conviction touches their peers. Words of condemnation only hurt and drive people away from the love of God in Christ. Thankfully, a generation is praying today. A move of God's power is at hand.

Remember, the great turning points in human history are often shrouded in the guise of insignificance. We are in the *small-beginnings* stage of something that will transform the nation. God often hides small beginnings for the sake of safety. The Exodus of Israel begins with the statement "and the baby cried."[70] The cry was from a baby hidden in a basket in the bulrushes of the Nile. The Christian faith begins with a baby in the manger.[71] A Baby was hidden in a rude manger in Bethlehem.

A simple prayer meeting in Antioch of Syria eventually impacted the Roman Empire and changed the face of Europe. Western civilization owes much to that seemingly insignificant event. It was in Antioch (Acts 13), the Holy Spirit spoke through praying teachers and prophetic intercessors. The charge was given to send out "Paul and Barnabas to the work to which I have called them." Even their mission had an incognito, enigmatic quality to it. The Holy Spirit Himself was mapping out the mission. The rest is history. Europe would be forever changed. Yet the revolution of the gospel message had small, almost untraceable beginnings. In Antioch, a multicultural congregation where the saints were first called Christians is where the evangelistic wave originated.

The Lord has staked His claim on today's youthful generation, both Jew and Gentile alike. He has put in them a fearless, brave heart. They are not afraid to face evil giants just as the shepherd lad David did. They know it only takes one knockout blow delivered to big Goliath and everything in the battle turns. It is very similar to the effect of falling dominoes at a Domino Topplers Tournament. When the first domino falls, the process of toppling dominoes continues until the very last one falls.

By God's grace, we established this mountain sanctuary to serve this generation of God seekers. They have a big vision for national deliverance.

They are up against bad odds. But you can count on, you can even bet on the little *Davids* of today. The Lord is on their side. That changes the equation. More importantly, the Lord of glory is in their hearts. "Christ in you the hope of glory" is a reality to them. They are serious about *mobilizing a multicultural, multigenerational solemn assembly in ceaseless worship and prayer for revival and cultural reformation in America.* (This is the sign they have painted in calligraphy on our Prayer Center wall.)

It is decision time in America. In fact, it is one minute till midnight! We hope and pray that we who are responsible stewards of this mountain will play some key role in pointing the nation to God. That is our persistent prayer.

For years, JoAn and I have sailed her pretty 22 foot Wellcraft Starwind sailboat named *Windsong* on the big lake below Prayer Mountain. We are always searching for the wind. JoAn observes flags and the swaying of tree branches. As soon as we motor away from the marina docks, JoAn has her eyes on the telltales hanging from her sails. She is ever searching across the waters of the big lake for wave ripples, known as cat's-paws. As a sailor, she is always seeking the wind. A sailor knows if you can find the wind, you can find power. You can find movement. Today we are ever seeking the wind of the Spirit. We go where it is blowing. There have been times we felt the church was standing still, like a becalmed boat with no wind in its sails.

Today the wind of the Holy Spirit is blowing. Now is the time to unfurl our sails. It's time to move, to blow and go with the blowing wind of God.

The story of Prayer Mountain will be continued through the lives of the current and future people at Mountain Creek Church. All things are possible for people of prayer. They know that nothing is too hard for God. The Lord unlimited reigns forever.

If this mysterious mountain could speak, it would tell of the glory of the Lord. Someday soon the mountains shall break forth into singing just as Isaiah the prophet prophesied, and all the trees of the field shall clap their hands.[72] Can you imagine what a monumental song that will be? For this, all creation groans. Nature is today in labor, travailing in birth pangs to bring forth a new earth wherein dwells righteousness. It is eagerly awaiting the dawning of the Day.

Then the hills will sing out in a grand chorale. All the trees of the wilderness will applaud. And the righteous, who are waiting for that Day, will shine like the sun.

*I can think of no better time than this to affirm the importance
and urgency of prayer for our nation and our world.*
–Billy Graham.

*The church and the world need nothing as much as a mighty spirit
of intercession to bring down the power of God on earth.
Pray for the Spirit of intercession to bring a great prayer revival.*
–Andrew Murray

*As it is written,
"Eye has not seen, nor ear heard,
Nor have entered into the heart of man
The things which God has prepared for those who love Him."*
1 Corinthians 2:9

*Learn from yesterday.
Live for today.
Hope for tomorrow.*
–Des Evans

AFTERWORD: A NOTE OF THANKS

*One thing that moves me much as I look back over my young days
is the fact that so many people have given me something
of value without their knowing it.*
–Albert Schweitzer

We were often amazed at the diverse sources of encouragement: Thanks to DeVern Fromke, author of *Unto Full Stature, Ultimate Intention,* and *Life's Ultimate Privilege* for his week spent in our home praying with us when we were preparing to launch this ministry.

Thanks to Leonard Ravenhill, revivalist and author of the classic *Why Revival Tarries,* and to his son David, for so much quality time and encouragement in the beginning years of this work.

Thanks to Chaplain (Col) John Powledge for his military records research concerning the liberation of Dachau Concentration Camp in World War II.

We will be forever grateful to Dr. James and Winnie Barnes for taking us in, a young family between assignments. The two years at Northeast Chapel as Youth Pastors were years of spiritual growth. While there, I began driving through these hills.

Thanks to the wonderful Lindsay family, Freda (Mom), Shira, Gilbert, and Dennis, for the privilege of working with the Christ for the Nations publications after the passing of their father, Gordon. Our season at that post brought us closer geographically to the mountain and to miracles. I often drove Mom Lindsay to significant national gatherings. She referenced me as "one of my boys."

Good friends like Dr. Alan Bryant and Sharon helped us begin this dream with many meetings in their home. Other families commuted across the county to help us—such as Jim and Sarah Yarbrough, Russell and Nancy Buckley. We owe them all gratitude.

Steve and Sharon Myers, who always remained faithful servants, helping in so many ways. Thank you both.

Thanks to Mike Wallace, the principal field engineer over the Mountain Creek neighborhood development, who offered us regular advice in our beginning days of construction. His big grin and congeniality showed us that he was genuinely concerned about us. He assisted us in reconfiguring our rough lane which led up the mountain.

Dr. Charles Tandy, M.D. was chief anesthetist at Dallas' Methodist Central Hospital—and a true Godsend. He was our local Dallas District 3 City Councilman as well. He and his wife Rowena were well-known Christian leaders in our town. Rowena was chairperson for a compassionate ministry to Dallas' hurting, homeless people, Dallas Life. Dr. Tandy often helped us navigate our way through the complex maze of Dallas City Hall's twenty-seven different departments. When Dallas Fire Department required us to install an expensive fire hydrant down on the city street, Dr. Tandy pointed out that our Eagle Ford Drive had no hydrants on its whole two mile stretch. Therefore, if ours were to be the only hydrant available to fire trucks, we should not bear the expense alone. In the end, Public Works installed it. We only had to pay one third the cost of installation. A much more reasonable burden.

From our earliest beginnings we were inspired to be a compassion ministry, sharing our bread with the hungry. Lovie Phillips and Elizabeth Brown, two lovely ladies, angels actually, whose husbands were missionary statesmen, inspired us to help their orphans in Uganda, Rwanda, Kenya, and other lands. They are known as "mama" to hundreds of children whom they have helped.

Thanks to Rod Butler, our spiritual son, who directs the children's ministry at DFW's popular KCBI Radio station, the brainchild of the late Dr. W.A. Criswell. Rod made the tough move from Wildwood to Dallas with us. He was always a fun, loving big brother to our son Kipling. God rewarded Rod with a beautiful wife and family.

Thanks to the late Bob Terrell, a dear apostolic friend. He was always wiser than he sounded, and ever full of loving encouragement.

Thanks to my Southern Dallas pastors and evangelists prayer and fellowship group. Their weekly encouragement and prayers always meant so much to me. Christ Jesus was always in our midst.

Thanks to our local community pastors alliance, coordinated by Keith Brister of Duncanville's First Baptist Church. Together we get things accomplished for God, such as aiding hundreds of New Orleans evacuees from Hurricane Katrina. JoAn and I are always heartened to realize that we do not labor alone in this community.

Thanks to Dr. Gary Cook, president of Dallas Baptist University, for his example of integrity and for sharing his bright and talented students with our fellowship.

Thanks to Stephen Evans of Light of Life International for training our youth to be compassionate ministers among the poorest of the poor in Central America.

Thanks to Daniel Aleman who directed *Oracion Explosivo* for years, holding monthly prayer and communion services for Hispanic leaders in our chapel. Because of *Oracion Explosivo*, we were blessed to enjoy a short, but quality time of fellowship with Dr. Billy Graham.

Thanks to our prayerful presbytery leaders. They are all seasoned men of God whose ministries have proved to be world changers. Their friendship and moral support have been of incalculable value. Thanks again, my brothers: Cleddie Keith, Des Evans, Rene Brown, Syvelle Phillips, and Jim Mackey. You have helped us stay in the arena fighting the good fight of faith.

TESTIMONIAL

This book is an encouraging compilation of faith, trial, a mountain man and a faithful God.

If The Mountain Could Speak: It would include the tale of a minister still new to DFW, who had turned over a successfully pioneered work in Ohio to obey the voice of God to come to Dallas/Fort Worth.

Like Abraham, we were going into a land we knew not. We were told that the Lord had angels that had gone before us that would meet and minister to us. Robert and JoAn would be two of those angels and Prayer Mountain would be a hosting birth chamber for a new work in DFW.

Upon meeting Robert Summers, there was an almost immediate kindred connection. The Lord gave this *mountain man* a love for me and me a love for him; this was God. Terri, my wife, and I were meeting in the homes of people the Lord began to gather unto us. We quickly outgrew their residences and had the need to settle in a stable place for Friday night prayer and vision casting. Robert opened the mountain and the current prayer room to us and received me like the priest of Nob received David. There David was offered refuge, food and the sword of Goliath; a giant-killing weapon.

This mountain, infused with many miracles, would be the high place from which we would launch. Mountain men are pioneers and mountain men attract mountain men. After three months of interest meetings we requested their Summit building for our official church inaugural meeting. We quickly grew and are now in our own lovely facilities in Arlington, TX.

I believe Isaiah 52:7 captures our meeting and relationship best: *How beautiful on the mountains* (Prayer Mountain) *are the feet of the messenger who brings good news, the good news of peace and salvation, the news that the God of Israel reigns!*

This book will speak to your soul and stir you to belief and action. I not only endorse this product, I'm a client.

Dr. Von Peaks,
Senior Pastor
Good News Intl. Christian Center

Endnotes

1 Quoted from JoAn's book *Keepers of the Treasure*, Prayer Mountain Press, Dallas

2 Robert McAmis, M.D. later became a solid Christian. He was the major benefactor of a related congregation in the Houston/LaPorte area, Life Community Church. JoAn and I phoned him to pray with him and thank him just three weeks before he passed away in December, 2009.

3 Psalm 103:7

4 Deut. 11:11,12

5 Genesis 28:16,17

6 Psalm 60:12

7 *Paths of Power*, Christian Publications, Harrisburg, PA, p. 13 Fall, 1985

8 Isaiah 55:11

9 From *The New King James Bible*, Nelson Publishers; Kingdom Dynamics comment on Isaiah 55:11

10 General Felix Sparks is quoted from his military log book which later was entered into the Congressional Record in a Subcommittee hearing about the shooting of SS Guards at Dachau.

11 Psalm 9:12

12 1 Corinthians 15:3-6 NIV

13 Ibid. v. 8

14 1 Corinthians 5:7,8

15 Romans 8:28

16 2 Corinthians 4:15, 16

17 Matthew 5:14

18 See Matthew 18:19 where Jesus is teaching on the essential need for agreement.

19 *I'll Be Somewhere Listening* by V.O. Stamps and J.B. Coats; Stamps-Baxter Music, Dallas, Texas

20 *Total Commitment to Christ*, p. 14, Christian Publications. Camp Hill, PA

21 London: Epworth Press. p. 22

22 2 Corinthians 7:6 Paul explains his despair and then comfort when his disciple Titus arrives to assist him.

23 *Through the Year With Samuel Chadwick*, London: Epworth Press. p 53

24 John 9:5

25 1 Corinthians 1:24

26 Ephesians 21:15, 16

27 Exodus 15:21

28 Genesis 19:27

29 Genesis 24:63

30 Genesis 28: 32

31 *Zion's Hill*, a hymn attributed to James Allen Crutchfield

32 Matthew 21:13

33 2 Corinthians 3:17

34 Exodus 15:21

35 Exodus 30:7,8

36 John 4:23

37 Revelation 5:8,9

38 Zephaniah 3:17

39 2 Chronicles 20:15

40 1 Corinthians 10:11

41 Joshua 1:11

42 2 Corinthians 4:9 Williams Version

43 Chesapeake Energy's Annual Report, 2010

44 1 Corinthians 15:57

45 *In Flanders Fields* by John McCrae, 1872-1918

46 Tozer is quoted from "The City" winter 2009, publication of Houston Baptist University in a reprint of a 1952 issue of an Alliance Weekly (Chicago) article *Playground or Battleground.*

47 2 Corinthians 3:17

48 1 Samuel 14:6

49 Matthew 18:19

50 1 Corinthians 9:26

51 *Born After Midnight,* Christian Publications, 1959, Harrisburg PA, p. 34

52 Romans 8:26,27

53 1 Samuel 15:22, 23 Amplified

54 *Born After Midnight* p. 42

55 Luke 18:1

56 Lamentations 3:26

57 Luke 6:12

58 Lamentations 3:22,23

59 Jeremiah 29:4,7 NIV

60 Jeremiah 29:10-14 NIV

61 Job 31:16, 17

62 1 Samuel 7:12

63 *Come Thou Fount of Every Blessing* by Robert Robinson

64 Isaiah 58:14

65 Zechariah 4:10

66 1 Samuel 17:50

67 1 Samuel 17:47

68 Acts 2:17, 18

69 Psalm 24:6

70 Exodus 2:6

71 Luke 2:7

72 Isaiah 55:12